Indian English Drama

A Gynocritical Perspective

Indian English Drama

A Gynocritical Perspective

Durgesh Ravande

ATLANTIC
PUBLISHERS & DISTRIBUTORS (P) LTD

Published by

ATLANTIC

PUBLISHERS & DISTRIBUTORS (P) LTD

7/22, Ansari Road, Darya Ganj, New Delhi-110002
Phones : +91-11-40775252, 40775214, 23273880, 23275880
Fax : +91-11-23285873
Web : www.atlanticbooks.com
E-mail : orders@atlanticbooks.com

Branch Office: Chennai
Phones : +91-44-48531784, 28291383
E-mail : chennai@atlanticbooks.com

Printed & bound in India by Atlantic Print Services

Dedicated to

The fond memories of my mother,
Late Sow. Mandabai,
who brought me on the stage of life
and taught to enact in various situations.

Preface

Indian English Drama has predominantly been an exposure of male tradition. In a country like India where glorious dramatic tradition is found, the presence of women from writing to directing a play is certainly exceptional. On the other hand, the presentation of a woman in the male playwrights has been restricted to misogyny. The conventional, stereotyped, partially analyzed image of Indian woman in male-dominated plays fails to reveal the world of woman's experience, and therefore female dramatic tradition is neglected and remains out of sight. In this way, women's drama has obtained a trivial attention throughout the history of Indian English Drama. The male dramatic tradition has produced distinguished figures such as Sri Aurobindo, Rabindranath Tagore, Pratap Sharma, Girish Karnad, Badal Sircar, Mohan Rakesh, Vijay Tendulkar and many others. But there is certainly a dearth of speculating figures in female dramatic tradition. It is true that women's theatre can be the most appropriate entity to demonstrate the authentic world of women. Therefore, drama as an art should explore the dimensions of women's world of experience.

Women's drama in India is not comparatively a popular, well-recognized entity. The Indian women playwrights are not equally in focus as compared with Indian women novelists and poets. Actually, drama is an effective medium to unearth distinct facets of human life. It enacts even the invisible zones of human mind. Being suppressed under patriarchy for centuries, women should have a great number of unheard expressions to divulge before the world. In this way, drama can be instrumental in demonstrating their unheard discourse.

The book highlights the unexplored portions of woman's life through gender-centred social reality, language and stage strategy in the selected plays of Bharati Sarabhai, Mahasweta Devi, and Manjula Padmanabhan to procure at large a gynocentric implication. It also formulates coherence among the women playwrights of different phases to illustrate the female tradition in India. Though the female tradition is not equally developed as male dramatic tradition, it generates all the possibilities to discover different unrevealed issues. In this way, the book focuses on the dimensions of woman's life in androcentric society. It follows Showalter's model of Gynocritics that emphasizes woman's social as well psychological liberation. The basis of illustration here is my doctoral thesis. Though it draws on my thesis, yet the pivotal purpose is to better my understanding of the aspects covered therein. The ordering of chapters has been done according to the central idea or theoretical aspect in the concerned chapter. The chapters articulate multiple aspects to bring out the overall state of women in Indian society. Though their ideological ground in these chapters differs from one to another, they conclude on the note of woman's pathetic condition and inability to get sufficient scope to outwit the situation. It has been assumed that woman's world view and the facets of Indian womanhood are helpful in making a comprehensive interpretation of woman's self and subjectivity in the phallocentric society. As the Western theatre became the centre of dominant culture, Indian women's theatre would be at the centre of the dramatic culture in India. The present book is a small venture in this regard.

The book will be useful for the students and teachers of English Literature, particularly Indian English Literature, Indian English Drama, Feminist Literature, and researchers in these fields.

Durgesh Bhausaheb Ravande

Acknowledgements

I take this opportunity at the outset to express my heartfelt thanks to my research guide, teacher par excellence Dr. Harihar Kulkarni for his careful observations, momentous reassurance, and outstanding critical insight.

I would like to express my sincere thanks towards the UGC for financial assistance. I am thankful to Shri Vijay Kumarji Katruwar, the President of Pathri Taluka Shikshan Prasarak Mandal, and Shri Balkishanji Chandak, the Secretary, for their constant inspiration. I am also thankful to Dr. A.B. Chindurwar, the Principal of my college, for his constant support. I have a sincere gratitude towards all my colleague-friends. My intimate friends Vishvadhar Deshmukh, Dattaji Mehetre and Bhagwat Pastapure are always there to trust and respond to my budding comprehension. I am beholden to them.

I wish to thank Dr. Ajay Tengse, Dr. Ramesh Dhage, Dr. Padmarani Rao, Dr. Rajkumar, Dr. Dilip Chavan, Dr. Haribabu, Dr. Keshav Deshmukh, Dr. Arvind Nawle, Dr. Mustajeeb Khan, Dr. I. Venkateshwarralu, Dr. Obula Reddy, and Dr. Mebel Fernandis for their direct or indirect cooperation. I feel great to mention the names of my friends, Dr. R.T. Bedre, Dr. Nagnath Totawad, Ajay Yadav, Raghvendra Bilolikar, Dr. D.P. Digole, Rajaram Waman, Dr. Rohidas Nitonde, Gulab Shaikh, Ashok Bhosikar, Gajanan Janakwade, and Amit Shesh for their frank arguments. I am grateful to Dr. Shailaja Wadikar for her support. My thanks are also due to the Librarians of colleges and universities, and their staff for making the sources available to me. To begin with, I would like to mention, K.K.M. College Library, Manwath; Ramesh Mohan Library, EFLU, Hyderabad; American College Library, SCILET, Madurai; Dhvanya Loka Library, Mysore;

S.R.T.M. University, Library, Nanded; Kolhapur University Library, Kolhapur; Pune University Library, Pune; NSD Library, New Delhi; Sahitya Academi Library, New Delhi; and OUCIP Library, Hyderabad.

I am also thankful to my father, Bhau, and my wife, Shilpa for their encouragement. My sweet cheerleaders Parth and Gargi for their 'quite' support. Last but not the least, I wish to thank Dr. K.R. Gupta and Mr. Harjeet Singh of Atlantic Publishers and Distributors Pvt. Ltd., New Delhi for their publishing efforts.

Durgesh Bhausaheb Ravande

Contents

1

Texts, Contexts, and Perspectives

> While Western theatre fragmented into opera, ballet and drama based on dialogue, Indian theatre (drama) maintains a composite form of singing, dancing, verse, prose dialogue, and rhetorical speech with elements of social criticism.
>
> —Jacob Srampickal

The present book illustrates gender-centred reality, psychodynamics of language and stage strategy in the selected plays of Bharati Sarabhai, Mahasweta Devi and Manjula Padmanabhan for a gyno-centric study of Bharati Sarabhai's *The Well of the People* (1943) and *Two Women* (1952), Mahasweta Devi's *Mother of 1084* (1973) and *Bayen* (1976) and Manjula Padmanabhan's *Lights Out* (1986) and *Harvest* (1997). Noted critic Raman Selden (1989: 13) argues: "...a woman's experience includes a different perceptual and emotional life; women do not see thing in the same ways as men, and have different ideas and feelings about what is important or not important". In this way, a study of woman's experience becomes pivotal to explore woman's world. The book foregrounds the gender, language, and techniques with a view to explore the spatial dynamics leading ultimately to ascertain woman's worldview. It highlights predominantly how womanhood is instrumental in shaping the creativity of these *avant-garde* playwrights. With the help of textual strategies employed by the playwrights; it uncovers the female voice in the selected plays. It strives to unearth how these playwrights have challenged the social construction of gender by deconstructing the supportive socio-cultural paradigms. These playwrights believe firmly that the gender is constructed to serve the purpose of supremacy in patriarchal society. Therefore, the objective of the book is to explore the self and language of women through perception of gender-based social reality to defy woman's conventional, stereotyped construction in male-dominated society and to make it an elaborative gynic realization in male-centred world. In this way, the model for criticism on women's writing, proposed by Elaine Showalter forms the nucleus. On the other hand, though women's theatre in India is a marginal entity, yet it has been an appropriate medium to raise women's issues and ascertain the world of their experience. Though the plays represent Indian context, the researcher has purposely choosen Western theoretical base for his elaborations due to lack of a systematic Indian theoretical paradigm. Indian Feminism has certain restrictions as it could not develop a literary theory to interpret women's texts. Hence, it is an experiment to contextualize division texts in Western theory.

Elaine Showalter (1985: 130), the renowned feminist critic, urges to challenge the age-old structure of literary study for the evaluation of a woman's text as it fails to count an authentic female experience. She states:

> As we see in the analysis, one of the problems of the feminist critique is that it is male-oriented. If we study stereotypes of women, the sexism of male critics, and the limited roles women play in literary history, we are not learning what women have felt and experienced, but only what men have thought women should be.

Thus, she introduces a model to study a woman's text differing diametrically from the conventional models of literary study with patriarchal orientations. But does not suggest any concrete therotical framework as far social and psychological liberation of a woman is concerned. Therefore, the writer has taken in consideration marxist, feminist and psycho-feminist principles to firm his interpretations. The prime concern of Gynocritics, to use her coinage, is to recognize the feminine subject matters in the works of women writers. She maintains that the literary history has neglected the female tradition completely. Therefore, she advocates an anti-phallocentric model. While emphasizing the iconoclastic nature of women's writing, she demands the reconsideration of issues related to women's lives by challenging and demolishing the values and institutions created by men. The women writers have been expected to deconstruct first the male-centred text and later reconstruct the female text with the help of real woman experience. It is difficult for the women writers to invent their language because they have chosen the language of men as the language of their literary expression. Hence, Elaine Showalter suggests four models of difference to estimate a woman's text. These models are: biological, linguistic, psychoanalytic and culture. The model Gynocritics, in this way, occupies significance to deconstruct the predominant androcentric paradigms and discover a woman-centred text.

The plays of Bharati Sarabhai fuse Indian womanhood with the changing socio-cultural dynamics. Mahasweta Devi, in her plays, explores the pathetic condition of women as mothers to disclose the aspects of social reality. She rather expects humane treatment to women in male-dominated society. Whereas Manjula Padmanabhan in her plays depicts the actual state of contemporary Indian woman leading ultimately to explore the austere socio-reality in a metro city like Mumbai. In this way, the selected plays have a relational significance. The plays deal with internal as well as external issues related to woman's life. The plays aim at making women aware of their strengths as well as weaknesses too. They disclose the fact that women alone can stop the inhumanity with them and relive themselves from the phallocentric injustice. The plays create a community art which helps for social change through self-awareness. To a great extent, one sees a woman's world containing dreams, memories and a rich inner life in these plays. They offer new modes of perception, determine the ways of empowerment, and depict the gender difference.

Gender and performance-centred evaluation of these plays has a logical consideration. There are complex identities of women constructed as well as projected in Indian Drama. Women have been caught in misogyny. They have been posed as sinister, strugglers or men's substitute. In the plays of Tagore, Aurobindo, and other major playwrights, there is a limited scope to explore the world of women. Thus, study of these playwrights prove to be less-supportive to uncover the woman's self and also the world of their experience. It is also necessary to redefine the reality because woman's social reality and experience has always been different from man's world of experience. It is believed that the women's writing qualitatively differs from writing by men on the basis of their experience as a woman. Therefore, Elaine Showalter (1985: 137) emphasizes the need to rebuild the past of women so that 'a woman's text' can be created. She asserts:

> Before we can even begin to ask how the literature of women would be different and special, we need to reconstruct its past, to rediscover scores of women novelists, poets, and dramatists whose work has been obscured by time, and to establish the continuity of the female tradition from decade to decade, rather from Great woman to Great woman.

The texts of women writers are largely denied when their experience connotes a radical realism. Chris Weedon (1987: 127) states: "Patriarchy implies a fundamental organization of power on the basis of biological sex, an organization which, from a poststructuralist perspective, is not natural and inevitable, but socially produced." In this way, the plays of women writers, to some extent, challenge the artificial world pillared on patriarchy. She adds further:

> Cixous's appropriation of Lacanian psychoanalysis is relatively optimistic about the possibility of transforming the patriarchal symbolic order through giving women a new sense of themselves, repressed until now, and asserting different feminine meanings and values at present repressed by patriarchy. (68)

The women characters in male-centred text appear mostly as an evidence of misogyny, victim of male desire, stereotyped image, falsehood or a dull, subsidiary record of women's oppression. The female text, otherwise, explores the different aspects of oppression related to the female self. It is crucial to find here that women are enjoying the pleasures of being women. The absolute pleasure for them lies in realization of womanhood and an attempt to create a zone for their expression.

The Indian women playwrights are at the juncture to perform a duel role—to deconstruct predominately the socio-cultural paradigms, and to reconstruct a female perspective and experience to challenge the stereotyped images. It has been observed that the socio-cultural construction of a woman does not go beyond being a sexual object. The patriarchal structure, in this way, creates an unsuitable and also unacceptable system for them. For example, Chandi in *Bayen*, Sujata in *Mother of 1084*, Jaya in *Harvest*, Frieda in *Lights Out*, Anuradha in *Two Women*, and old woman in *The Well of the People* are the prototypes of biased construction. But the playwrights challenge the indifference to strengthen the female voice and redefine the womanhood.

Drama combines the real and fictional art and presents the events and characters within a dimension of space and time. It has been a powerful form of education in social meanings and values, and also an effective analyzer of gender, class, and race beliefs. Being the oldest literary genre in India, drama has been playing a vital role in reshaping the socio-cultural milieu of this country. It is more powerful than fiction and poetry to initiate the practical change. Drama demonstrates perfectly the social relationship. It has been an instrument of social reformation in different parts of the world. In her introduction to the book *Staging Resistance*, Tutun Mukherjee (2005: 8) observes: "As a form, the drama is more public and social than other literary arts are." Drama is not merely a theory but a productive practice. It is the most appropriate medium to tackle the life-like issues and suggest an acceptable solution. Neither poetry nor fiction has proved any practical essence in shaping the model of an ideal society as compared to drama with its advanced expressive forms.

The American Heritage Dictionary of the English Language defines drama as "a prose or verse composition intended for representation by actors, impersonatriate the characters and performing the dialogue and action". It is a literary composition involving conflict, action, crisis and atmosphere designed to be acted by players on a stage before the audience.

India has a rich dramatic tradition in the form of the classical Sanskrit theatre. It has been the perennial source for skillful performances in different parts of the country. The Indian plays have been staging effectively the socio-cultural dynamics of Indian life. But to a great extent, woman has been subordinated in different formats of dramatic art. Her image is either substituted or neglected. The issues of women are rarely represented even though women perform an important role in different walks of life. The male dominance rather discourages the talented women writers in India to single out drama as their literary domain. Drama is the most effective medium of interaction with the masses.That's why, it is a crucial social discourse. But the issues of Indian women have rarely been found any place in these plays. On the other hand, the women writers in India have been reluctant to choose drama for their literary expression. There are a few women playwrights in the country who could acclaim the recognition of the masses. Actually, woman writer has potential to tackle the gender issues. Taking the fact into consideration, the plays of these three women playwrights have been chosen here for a comprehensive study.

The book is divided into five chapters. Chapter 1 is an introductory. It studies the woman, society and the use of techniques in Indian English Drama. The sections in this chapter are divided further into study of male tradition and female tradition. Chapter 2 discovers social reality prior to gender construction. Chapter 3 explores the psychodynamics of woman's language. Chapter 4 incorporates the study of techniques in the selected plays to focus how these women playwrights differ from their male counterparts in demonstrating pivotal issues of self and subjectivity. Chapter 5 is a critical synopsis of the arguments made in the earlier chapters. It discusses the theatrical and dramatic merits of these plays and focuses on the contribution of these playwrights in the formation of a new society.

The dramatic tradition in India has its origin in classical Sanskrit drama. It is *fons et origo* of literature in India. Indian drama owes to the classical Sanskrit drama in several respects. Talking about the origin of drama, Adya Rangacharya (1971: 3) comments: "...the theatre may have come into existence almost with men". S. Levis (2005: 7) claims: "The Sanskrit theatre is the Indian theatre par excellence." The classical Sanskrit dramatic practices reinforce a noteworthy past to Indian theatre. The Sanskrit plays represent Indian society and culture. In the words of A.B. Keith (2005: 7), Sanskrit theatre is "the highest product of Indian poetry...summing up in itself the final conception of literary art achieved by the very self-conscious creators of Indian literature." In other words, the Sanskrit theatre fortifies the basic dramatic development in the country. The Sanskrit plays, in short, trace the need to produce "an ananda-blissful pleasure that would lead the mind towards the state of Sthayibhava or equipoise" (Rangacharya: 13). The dramatists, viz. Bhasa, Kalidasa, Bhavabhuti, Sudraka, Vishakhadatta, and Harsha were among the prominent practitioners of Sanskrit plays.

Bharatmuni's *magnum opus*, *Natyashastra,* is the first ever text on dramaturgy. It deals with 'the laws of performance'. *Natyashastra,* precceder to Aristotle's *Poetics,* is the only book of its kind for centuries. It was composed in short versical metre—*Shloka*. It is not merely an abridgement of original voluminous text of Lord Brahma but a liberal reconstruction of the original. The text lays down the bedrock of dramatic presentation. The original work is significantly reconstructed by Bharata. In course of time, a number of changes were introduced by the modifiers of this work. The text of *Natyashastra*, available today, has thirty-seven chapters with 5,569 verses. *Natyashastra* has almost been reckoned as the foundation of science of dramaturgy. Adya Rangacharya in his celebrated text *The Indian Theatre* does not assign the authorship of this work to any particular writer for its unconcrete structure. *Natyashastra* lays down the theory of drama as its fundamental objective. It presents an ideal code of conduct for audio-visual production. The two-fold function assigned to drama, i.e. to instruct and to entertain has been mentioned here for the first time in the history of Indian drama. Adya Rangacharya's (1971: 15) following observation formulates the position of Bharata's text: "The Indian is not only one theatre of the subcontinent but is also a tradition that has survived all the upheavals of political and cultural history. That is the achievement of Bharata and his *Natyashastra*."

The appropriate study of *Natyashastra* is possible in the light of generic term Roopka only. It is almost expected that a dramatic work should be an imitation of men and their doings. In other words, it must be a roopka of their respective lives. Any dramatic work should essentially perform the real life. Bharata's *Natyashastra* avows the use of speech, gestures, movements and intonation. Bharata is fully aware of different representative modes. These modes are further divided into four major types. These four types or *Vritis* are as follows:

Bharati Vriti – Pre-dominance of speech and poetry
Arabhati Vriti – Predominance of actions

Kaishki Vriti – Predominance of dance and music
Sattvattiss Vriti – Predominance of emotions.

Thus, *Natyashastra* elaborates the how and what of drama. It also provides a proper guideline for dramatic presentation. Bharata gives minute details of presentation in this seminal text.

As far the characterization in the classical Indian theatre is concerned, woman has been presented as a beautiful, loyal and honest substitute of man. The theatre strived to enact rather divinity in women characters. She was shown as a worshiper, God-fearer but not as a strong, bold or rebellious. On the other hand, the plays represent the religious society of its time in which a woman has a trivial role to perform. The folk theatre popularized after classical theatre, to some extent, favoured women's socio-cultural stature for the performance.

II

The folk theatre began to obtain 'a popular choice' to the end of sixteenth century in different parts of the country. It borrowed certain stage devices from the classical Sanskrit drama. Actually, the decline of classical Sanskrit drama marks the growth of folk theatre. The folk theatre obtained the praise of masses and started growing rapidly in both quality and quantity. The folk forms, in a truer sense, reflect the country's linguistic, cultural, and religious diversity. The folk performances in different parts of the country were interlinked with each other on the basis of their attempt to interlink the individual truth with the universal truth. In this way, it ascertains a momentous position in the history of Indian

Drama. Vasudha Dalmia (2006: 160) comments: "...delving into folklore meant tracing the past roots of a given culture." Her observation expounds a link between folklore and culture of the country. The various dramatic performances started taking place in preceding centuries. On the other hand, the Bhakti cult helped substantially for the origin and growth of folk performances in different parts of the country to the end of nineteenth century.

Raymond Williams (2006: 155) rightly observes: "(f)olk in this period had the effect of backdating all elements of popular culture, and was often offered as a contrast with modern popular forms, either of a radical and working class or of a commercial kind." In this way, he illustrates the growth of folk performances in India.

Dance plays an important role in any folk performance. The folk performance has been given a dramatic aspect with the help of prosic dialogue. The most important part of any folk play is the picturesque make-up and the colourful costumes. The folk performance obtains a respective place in the Indian social life by representing the culture, politics, and society with a wider consideration. The folk performances originated during this phase are: Ramlila, Raslila and Nautanki of North, Bhavai of Gujarat, Tamasha of Maharashtra, Jatra of Bengal, Ånkignat of Assam, Yakashgana of Karnataka, Veethi Natakamu and Burrakatha of Andhra and Thurukoothu of Tamil Nadu. The respective cultures and society have a significant position in these regional performances.

On the other hand, the folk theatre failed to raise the issues of women, to a great extent. The purpose of woman character in any folk performance was restricted to entertainment only. In this way, woman's image received a negative representation in various folk presentations. She has been depicted as a dissolute, deserted creature. On the other hand, women were not allowed to be a part of any performance. In most of the folk performances, woman was portrayed as a mute follower of men.

III

The women tradition in Indian English Drama seems to be marginal till the late half of the twentieth century. Actually, the ideology of gender is shaped most particularly in the discourses such as talking, writing and enacting. In this way, women should have a close association with drama. But their response remained marginal as far the dramatic performances are concerned. Elaine Showalter observes: "Each generation of women writers has found itself, in a sense, without a history, forced to discover the past anew, forging again and again the consciousness of their sex." On the other hand, the textual strategies and the use of language help indeed to uncover the female tradition of writing in India.

The women's liberation movement in India began after a few decades of the Independence. The right to vote was obtained in Cochin and Travancore considerably earlier of the Independence. Sarojini Naidu, the first woman president of Congress (1925) commenced women's participation in national movement through her lead role in Salt March. But it took a great deal of time to find women's direct participation in different walks of life. The creative writers in our country dealt with malignant images, myths and stereotypes related to woman's self. The issues of women received a diminishing attention and representation. The image of a woman in earlier phase was restricted to: "a chaste virgin or as an embodiment of sin and imperfection" (Singh: 1). It took a few years more to deconstruct the stereotyped image of woman in Indian literature. The women novelists of this phase were content to portrait woman either as a suffering wife or a restricted widow. The trapped image of woman in literature was a reflection of social trauma received for centuries. The male-creative writers, on the other hand, were careful enough to personify the women characters as helpless, dejected, and marginalized. The women were not allowed to play any kind of role in socio-political affairs. The quandary of women, for the very first time in Indian history, became a public affair with the help of literature of this period.

Being a dialogic form; drama is more suitable for women's expression. There should be an expression of their bodily experience in performances. But the women tradition in Indian English Drama denotes a different fact. The women remained invisible in their visibility for a long time in the history of Indian

English Drama. They happened to speak in a male-controlled language. That's why, the fact is that there were a very few women playwrights before and after some decades of the Independence who could voice the realistic condition of women through their plays. Their participation in dramatic art was restricted to choreograph a dance or assist the male directors.

Street theatre, one of the powerful folklorist forms, transmuted, to some extent, the issues of women on a larger social canvas. Anita Singh (2009: 2) observers: "...street theatre had emerged as a strong medium for highlighting women's issues and exclusive forum where women audiences could relate the issues." The decades of the eighties and nineties have been crucial in this regard. The different reasons directly or indirectly related to the subordinate position of women in society could get a direct accordance in Indian Drama. Strangely, the forum working for women's stature was restricted for a long time to the involvement of women. The dramatic participation of Indian women was nobody's concern for a long time. Meanwhile, feminist theatre emerged as an instrumental branch of drama. But the feminist theatre is not a separate entity in India. "It was born out of an interaction between experimental theatre movement of the 1960s and the feminist movement of this time" (*ibid.*). It initiates a strong protest against male ideology for restricting over two millennia the women performances. A drama researcher often gets confused indifferentiating between feminist theatre and womanist theatre. Susan Bassnett's (1984: 15) observation in this regard makes the overhead point clear. She states:

> Feminist Theatre logically bases itself on the established concerns of the organized Women's Movement, the seven demands: equal pay; equal education; and job opportunities; free 24-hour nurseries; free contraception and abortion on demand; financial and legal independence and end to discrimination against lesbians and a woman's right to define her own sexuality, freedom from violence and sexual coercion....

To put in nutshell, feminist theatre widely differs from womanist theatre. Like Women's Liberation Movement, it argues for over all freedom of women of different social classes.

The late nineteenth century marks a beginning of women playwrights' contribution to Indian English Drama. The earlier contribution was not quite noteworthy. Except Bharati Sarabhai's two plays, viz. *The Well of the People* and *Two Women* there is not any significant contribution to this genre before Independence (excluding Mrinalini Sarabhai's *Captive Soil*).

Mrinalini Sarabhai is a celebrated dancer and choreographer. She obtains an unmatched reputation as a classical dancer. Her dance dramas celebrate the Indian womanhood. Her worldview, to a greater extent, retains the essence of humane values. She is the founder-director of Darpana Academy of Performing Arts, Ahmedabad. Her unparallel contribution to Indian classical dance ensured many national and international awards and citations to her credit. She is called as 'The High Priestess of Indian Dance.' Mrinalini Sarabhai gave a fresh perspective to Indian classical dance. Chaman Ahuja (2001: 16) asserts: "Mrinalini makes no difference between dance and drama; convinced that the two are twin sisters, she believes that she has been doing plays all her life." She has choreographed over three hundred dance-dramas in her lifetime. Her writing includes novels, poetry, plays and stories for children. To be précis, "the syntax of her creativity mediates between a moral commitment to traditional form and the desire to claim one's own experiments as unique, unrepeatable".

Her play *The Captive Soil* (1945) brings together the actions and reactions of various social groups during the freedom movement. It has a prologue and an epilogue. The play follows the Western dramatic technique and presents a conflict "between the ruthless imperialist authority and the rising will of the Indian people to become a free nation" (Gupta: 71). The first act is The Outside whereas the second is The Inside. S.K. Bhatta (1980: 41) argues: "*Captive Soil* is a powerful verse-play in two acts with a Prologue and an Epilogue, presenting the actions and reactions found among different sections of our country during the movement." The play presents particularly different levels of authority. These different levels of authority are presented in the first act of the play. The second act portrays the characters unable to free the nation from the clutches of the Britishers. *The Captive Soil* is thus "a small, premising play which attempts to bring to life the conflict between the callous brutalities of the imperialist" (Gupta: 73). The play can be studied as an intense urge for freedom. The playwright intends to focus on social reality of her time. She emphasizes also the role of women in freedom movement. The women played an important role in the movement but could receive a modest attention. Mrinalini Sarabhai discovers the female aesthetic in the present play. The play is a smaller part in the female dramatic tradition in the country. The women showed an interest in the Freedom Movement out of a strong desire for their personal liberation. But the freedom of the nation brought a partial fulfillment to their expectations. Even after the freedom, women could not rescue themselves from patriarchal notions of slavery. Mrinalini Sarabhai develops the female tradition through this play, as she tackles, the issue of women's liberation.

One more woman playwright deserves to be mentioned is Swarnakumari Devi Ghosal. Her play *Princess of Kalyani* is an allegorical presentation. Kalyani is an embodiment of goodness and beneficence. She is the princess of Devagiri. The wicked brother of queen instigates people against king to occupy the throne but Dhruvakumar, a sincere soldier of the king, hampers his attempt.

The noble characters like Kalyani, the King, and Hashi are presented in the play with a great reverence to their nobility. On the other hand, the wicked characters such as the Queen and Matangini are the embodiments of jealous and abhorrence. The playwright presents here good woman as princess Kalyani and bad as the queen. The playwright shows her concern for a logical difference between good and evil. The differences at the level of characters are not merely individualistic but representatives of differing human tendencies. The play, to a greater extent, unfolds a family conflict as it focuses on the family crisis. The balance between two different types of characters is highly appreciative. The playwright is keen to prototype the different human tendencies as a part of social reality. The language used in the play shows the difficulty of the playwright in breaking the conventional linguistic strategy. The play slightly helps to extend the female tradition because women's model of writing is not its supporting basis.

K.B. Thakur contributed *Mother and Child*, a three-act play. The play substantially borrows from *Mahabharata*, the great epic. The bond of relationship is the message of the play. The play takes us to this great epic to present a relational bond between a mother and her son. The play won Bhavan's Journal Prize for its brilliant presentation. The careful handling of the plot is praiseworthy here. Mother's affection for her child is not socially permitted when she is a *kumari mata* (mother without marriage). The play elaborates, in this way, an aspect of social reality. Mother's heart, to the end, conquers over artificial or man-made odds. The social law does not accept a mother's natural urge. The play ends on the note that a mother though having affection and sentiments for her own child, should mind well for the social codes of conduct, first. It remains 'a cry in wilderness' if she fails to do it. The subordination of woman in social convictions is interrogated here with an utmost priority to the actual state of women in Indian society. The play is a prototype of a woman's subordinate state in Indian society of pre-Independence phase.

The first act is about maiden Kunti's curiosity to test the boon. She gives birth to a son but fails to perform her duties as a mother. Her failure in doing it is an outcome of conventional social perspective which does not allow any woman becoming mother without being married.

The second act powerfully depicts a mother's suffering after being forced to hide the birth of Karna. Naturally, it is difficult for any mother to deny motherhood out of social constraints. The outpourings of her motherly heart resonate: "A mother's heart trembles for the safety of her sons who alone are her life" (Thakur: 43). The play is an example of the ancient social system. The women playwrights in our country seem to be concerned in presenting the issues through their plays that directly or indirectly explore a woman's self. Compared to the other plays discussed in this section, the present play essentially represents woman's language. The playwright attempts to deconstruct the age-old social values with the help of a revolutionary expression.

Arati Nagarwala captures readers' attention with her play *The Bait*. The play was written in 1969. It is divided into three acts. It deals with the unpolluted loyalty of an aboriginal villager and his love for natural justice. The villager takes an oath to kill the lion due to deadly attack on his wife. He shows his determination in following words:

SONA : (Puzzled) Yes, father. More...than you?

PANNA : But we will win. Together, we willout think him. (Nagarwala: 11)

He offers his own son as bait and plans to take his revenge against the lion. Panna, the villager, kills the lion and gets arrested by police for his crime. Arati Nagarwala follows the model of classical Sanskrit drama to a great extent. The reader comes across writer's prudence as a playwright with the clever use of reportage technique in the play. Her use of folk elements is also decisive. The playwright never uses sutradhara, though she follows the classical norms.

The civilized people, living particularly in urban parts of the country show complete negligence towards the tribals. The playwright finds something incredible with the tribal hence she urges to focus on the same. She mentions: "We are too self-centered, we lack the glorious old-fashioned virtu-loyalty... (like) "Panna's loyalty to his wife, Sona's to his father and the loyalty of entire village to one of their own..." (33). The other characters like Mukhra and Pookhroo are also important in the play. Apart from certain qualities; lack of suspense, staging limitations are the shortcomings of the play. The play certainly fails to develop woman's language. The central woman character has a male-centred perception that comes out as a part of social value.

Kamala Subramanian's attempt of merging two epics, i.e. *Ramayana* and *Mahabharata* to focus the neglected facts related to the life of two women characters—Gandhari and Kaikeyee, is definitely first ever attempt in the history of Indian English Drama. Writer's imaginative ability and gender concern are the most striking features of the play—*Gandharee and Kaikeyee*. Both the queens belong to two different yugas. They meet at a particular place and denote their personal standpoint. Kaikeyee tells Gandharee that how Mandhara changed her mind after listening the news of Rama's coronation. Mandhara forced her to demand fourteen years exile for Rama and also Bharata's coronation. Kaikeyee clarifies her side by showing her innocence in this matter. On the other hand, Gandharee displays her innocence as she justifies her doing. According to her, she always liked Pandavas. She had not any prejudiced views about them. Being mother of Kauravas, it was natural to care them more than Pandavas. History defamed her, as she mentions, without understanding properly her side. The playwright points out here that both of the queens were the victims of circumstances. The playwright's attempt to put forth the undiscovered self of these two historical characters shows her concern for the historically injustified characters. The interpretation of both these women characters is based more on male-centred ethos. The noted feminist critic Julia Kristeva observes that the values of women are always different than the values of men. In this way, the most of women characters in the history largely experienced partiality as their values are imposed rather chosen.

Mid-twentieth century onwards more women writers started showing their interest in drama. Among them, Dina Mehta and Poile Sengupta luminate Indian stage with their spark. Unlike the earlier women playwrights, they have a forceful expression and also revolutionary potentials. They deny the male-centred frame of writing and construct their works on genuine female experience. Both the playwrights have been taking sufficient efforts to structure a woman's text. The contemporary political, social reality is conveyed in their plays through different levels of meaning.

Dina Mehta began her career in journalism. It took some years to begin her carrier in drama. She began it with a radio play *Brides are not for Burning* (1979). The play received an international acclaim due to its contemplation for a burning social issue. The play is based on a sample dowry case. The social evil of dowry is yet prevalent in Indian society. The cases of dowry victims are enormous. Even after sixty-six years of Independence, there is not any considerable decrease in the number of victims.

According to CNN, Indian police receives more than 2,120 reports of death per year. The Government of India passed Dowry Prohibition Act but the dowry deaths could not be prevented. The playwright shows her protective mood in the play. The play is about Laxmi—a dowry victim's tragic end. She was ill-treated by her in-laws to such an extent that she commits suicide. The evildoers even try to suppress the very cause behind the suicide to avoid defamation. They manage law and try to deprive the attention of police. It happens almost in every dowry case when the parents of victim are helpless to do anything against these 'messengers of death'. The play never ends on the note of injustice with Laxmi as the playwright signifies Malini's (Laxmi's sister) voyage to unearth the actual motive behind her sister's death. She decides to fight for the justice of many Laxmis around by completing her law education. The playwright, suggests skillfully, a way to stop the evils like dowry system here. Malini becomes the voice of voiceless. Dina Mehta's other play *Getting Away with Murder* centres around the lives of three friends Mallika, a successful entrepreneur, Sonali with neurosis from childhood abuse, Razia, the gynecologist, whose husband has just brought an another wife. These unfortunate characters get support from each other in their difficulty of life. The interpretation of women-centred issues in Dina Mehta's plays is realistic and it provides enough space to study the life of Indian middle-class women on the basis of their psychological and social state.

Uma Parmeshwaran being a prominent contemporary woman dramatist contributes this genre with *Sons Must Die*—a play based on 1947 partition *Meera* (1971), *Sita's Promise* (1981), *Dear Deedi* (1980), *My Sister* (1989). *Rootless but Green are the Boulevrd Tress* (1998)—All of these plays were published in her collection, *Sons Must Die and Other Plays* in 1998 as a part of South Asian Canadian Literature Series (SACLIT). *Sons Must Die* exposes the experience of three women in 1947 India. The play depicts the horrors of war and it is set in the backdrop of Indo-Pak war. Three mothers from different parts of India: A Tamil Brahmin, Zohara Begum—a Muslim Mother, and Prem Behn a Punjabi mother. They all meet at Kashmir in search of their sons.

A prominent figure among the contemporary Indian English playwrights, Poile Sengupta wrote her first play in 1993. Though the themes, style, and language of her plays vary from one play to another. There is a uniformed concern in her plays regarding the place of woman in Indian society. In this way, her dramatic art becomes 'woman-centred'.

The play *Mangalam* (1993) deals with a socially relevant subject. The play is within a play but with a special treatment. Sengupta uses the same characters to present different situations in different locations to illustrate the disturbing similarity. In this way, the play delineates the unchanged plight of Indian woman in family. The Indian woman from a small village, town, or metropolitan city, lives with a marginal difference as far her domestic and social status is concerned. The play *Mangalam* is significant for its stylistic. Her next play, *Inner Laws* (1994) is the best example to illustrate the relational difference. The play is also significant for its frequent allusions to Indian epics. *Keats was a Tuber* (1996) mocks at the use of English by Indians. The play *Alipha* (2001) is a personal tragedy. It illustrates the changing context of relationship. In comparison to her other plays, *Thus Spake Shoorpanakha, So Said Shakuni* (2001) is more powerful in expression. It is a bold attempt to merge the two great Indian epics to explore the theme of desire and revenge. The two characters in the play, without any particular identity, represent their respective gender.

Poile Sengupta occupies a distinguished position in contemporary Indian Engilsh drama particularly for her socio-political rumination of contemporary Indian life. She is also keen to explore the world of contemporary Indian woman. In this way, she is one of the prominent Indian women playwrights divulging the issues of Indian woman with a priority.

IV

Bharati Sarabhai, the pioneering Indian woman playwright authored two plays, i.e. *The Well of the People* and *Two Women.* She depicts in her plays the emerging socio-cultural reality and dimensions of Indian womanhood. Her plays envisage the phase of thinking-transmutation. The protagonists of both these plays are certainly on the way of obtaining social ideality. The women protagonists are not enough confident initially to take their personal decisions like those of Dina Mehta's and Manjula Padmanabhan's protagonists. Yet, old woman in *The Well of People* and Urvashi in *Two Women* show certain signs of maturity in their thoughts leading them to individual actions. The old woman introspects thoroughly before transmuting her religious faith with the help of newly-awakened Gandhian social idealism. The psychological transformation, she undergoes, takes a great deal of time. In this way, she represents the dilemma of millions of Indian women who struggle for self-decision. The conventional faith does not allow old woman to reach easily any satisfactory conclusion. Anuradha in *Two Women* whereas tries to escape herself from conventional duties of Indian wife with the help of her friend Urvashi. On the other hand, Mrinalini Sarabhai portrays women characters in her *The Captive Soil* but in a restricted manner. Some other women playwrights such as Shri Devi, J.B. Billomoria and Arati Nagarwala were contain to present women characters in a conventional way. Most of the time, the characters were drawn from great epics like *Ramayana* and *Mahabharata* without modifying their individuality. The women characters in these plays are not capable enough to ask their rights or to take cudgel in their hands to change the predominant social order. But attempting drama as an expression of their creative genius is certainly appreciable. Though they never produced any tour de force; encouraged the women writers of twentieth century to attempt this genre. They boosted also the loyalty with this most effective medium of social change. During those days the means of social communication were scanty. Among the limited media, drama was the most crucial. Drama is certainly capable to serve the purpose of being an entertainer and also an instructor. The women playwrights proved it through their instrumental elaborations.

The last four to five decades of the twentieth century have brought some incredible changes in women's writing in India. The creative expression of these writers can be found in novels and poetry. The contemporary women writers like Dina Mehta, Manjula Padmanabhan, Poile Sengupta, and Mahasweta Devi have been serving their social cause with the help of drama. Hence, their dramatic voice is poignant. The women protagonists of their plays are strong and capable enough to perform their responsibilities. They attempt to look at society in general and woman in particular with a different perspective. I.D. Sharma (2004: 13) aptly puts: "Mahasweta Devi looks at women from the new angle of reality as humane with self-respect, rights, dreams, despairs, weakness, and strength." The endeavour of these contemporary dramatists is surely responsive. The stature of Indian woman in a phallocentric society finds a central position in the plays of these writers. The gender perception of Indian women playwrights is based on this social reality. On the other hand, the male dramatic tradition of pre-Independence phase signifies a marginal scope for the women's issues.

V

The Indian English Drama of pre-Independence phase consists either the influence of Western canon or William Jones, H.H. Wilson, and Sylvain Levi discovered, the National Theatre of Hindus. The First Indian Drama in English was written in 1831. Krishna Mohan Banerjee wrote the pioneering play *The Persecuted* or *Dramatic Scenes Illustrative of the Present State of Hindu Society in Calcutta*. It is a social play, depicting the Brahmin tricks to cheat the common people. Later on, Michael Madhusudan Dutt, the famous poet translated his three Bengali plays into English. His translated plays are: *Ratnavali* (1858), *Sermista* (1859), and *Is This Called Civilization?* (1871). The phase (1831-1974) was dominated by the male dramatists, except one or two women playwrights such as Bharati Sarabhai. The playwrights of this phase were divided in two groups, i.e. Major Playwrights and Minor Playwrights. The playwrights like Sri Aurobindo, Rabindranath Tagore, T.P. Kailasam and Harindranath Chattopadhyaya were the major playwrights of this phase.

Sri Aurobindo (1872-1950) is the leading contributor as far male dramatic tradition of this phase is concerned. The plays of Aurobindo fall particularly in the category of Complete Plays and Incomplete Plays. His complete plays are: *Perseus the Deliverer*,

Vasavadutta, *Rodogune*, *Viziers of Bassora*, and *Eric*. On the other hand, *The Witch of Ilmi*, *The Maid in the Mill*, *The Birth of Sin* and *Prince of Edur* are among his incomplete plays. The impact of great Sanskrit playwrights like Bhasa, Kalidasa and Bhavabhuti can be perceived on Aurobindo's plays. But K.R. Srinivas Iyengar (2007: 226) observes "...all five plays are steeped in poetry and romance, recalling the spirit and flavour of the distinctive dramatic type exemplified in different ways by Bhasa, Kalidasa and Bhavabhuti—though, of course, all have Aurobindonian undertones." The plays of Sri Aurobindo fuse different elements for a dramatic situation. It is a perfect depiction of different cultures and countries in various epochs. The modes and sentiments are essential in Aurobindo's plays. His plays are either tragedies or comedies. Among his complete plays only *Rodogune* is a tragedy. The element of romance in most of his plays is decisive. Aurobindo romanticizes the subject of his plays. While talking about the impression on Aurobindo's writing, K.R. Srinivas Iyengar rightly points out: "Sri Aurobindo draws numerous sources ranging from ancient Greek poets to Kingsley" (151). The issue of slavery of his own people under the foreign rule is depicted clearly in the plays of Sri Aurobindo. He incorporates the myth and legend to serve the purpose of revealing the aspects of social reality. His social intention makes his people aware of the British tyranny. On the other hand, the women characters in the plays of Aurobindo are restricted to the romantic flavour only. There is a mixture of Indian and Western stage strategies in the plays of Aurobindo. The vast learning of various subjects is undoubtedly presented in Aurobindo's plays and the use of language, presentation of scenes is among the dominant features of his plays.

The pre-Independence phase of Indian English Drama is largely contributed through translation. Rabindranath Tagore is among those writers who enriched Indian English Drama with their translated plays. His plays are a paradigm of Indian village life. There is an illustration of village power structure in most of his plays. His translated plays are *Sanyasi, Malini, Sacrifice, The King and The Queen, The Mother's Prayer, Somaka Ritvika, Chitra* and *The Water-fall.* The plays of Tagore mainly centralize religious, epic, legendary and political themes. The use of poetry is the most significant feature of his dramas. Tagore shows a considerable interest in following T.S. Eliot and W.B. Yeats popularized Poetic Drama as far his dramatic art is concerned. Bharati Sarabhai, the woman dramatist of this phase, followed the similar dramatic form in *The Well of the People*.

Tagore's celebrated play *Sanyasi* or *The Ascetic* is the English version of the original Bengali work, *Prakaritir Pratishodh*. According to Tagore (1997: 2), the play should be looked as "an introduction to the whole of my future literary work, or rather this has been the subject on which all my writings have dwelt—the joy of attaining the infinite with the finite." In *Malini*, Tagore deals with the conflict between old and new ethic. Noted critic and writer K.R. Srinivas Iyengar (1973: 130) remarks: "Malini is indeed new revelation, as in her own day and in her own way Joan the Maid was in France." The playlet *Chitra* draws its theme from *Mahabharata*, the great epic. Tagore highlights here "the idea that the real feminine beauty in Chitra alone could win Arjuna and not her borrowed beauty" (136). The playlet simply relates this legendary story with Tagore's feminine concern.

Tagore has a remarkable significance in the world of drama for his poetic presentation. The classical Sanskrit drama was renewed by Tagore. He, like other male playwrights of the phase, showed a slight significance to the women characters. Therefore, his women characters are subordinated or stereotyped in their appearance. Altogether, the women characters in his plays stand at the periphery. They are not crucially highlighted in his plays.

Tyagaraja Paramsiva Kailasam, a Kannada playwright, occupies a prominent place in the firmament of Indian English Drama. The plays of T.P. Kailasam breathe a deep reverence for an ancient culture and values of life. He links the legendary epics like *Ramayana* and *Mahabharata* with the contemporary situation out of his simon-pure social consideration. Like Tagore, Kailasam too shows a great deal of interest in representation of Indian society, culture and myth through his plays. The most poignant feature of Kailasam's plays is the blend of vision and stage craft. He wrote the plays, viz. *The Burden* (1933) *The*

Purpose (1944), *Fulfillment* (1944), *The Curse/Karma* (1948), and *Keechaka* (1945). He wrote thirteen playlets in his career.

The fusion of myth with contemporary life is perfect in Kailasam's plays. His play *Monologue* portrays woman as the eternal sufferer and man as the conventional consoler. The woman in his plays never goes beyond her conventional image. Besides, Aurobindo, Tagore and Kailasam, Harindranath Chattopadhayaya is also known for his social, historical and devotional plays. He wrote the plays, viz. *The Saint, The Sleeper Awakened, The Parrot, Jayadev, Sakubai, Raidas, Tukaram, Chokamela* and *Eknath*. He is known for his playlets of different types also. His plays are symbolic, didactic and propagandistic in nature. The use of allegory in his playlets is crucial. Chattopadhayaya advocates the need of social discrimination in his plays. The social plays of Harindranath Chattopadhyaya as K.R. Srinivas Iyengar comments: "manifestos of new realism" (27). His play *The Window* offers a bitter commentary on the conflict between capitalists and labourers. The playwright stands in the protest of the exploited workers who are forced to bear extreme difficulties under the cruel industry dominance of industrialists. *The Parrot* interrogates the age-old marriage institution in our country. A woman is compelled to tolerate cruelty under the working of injustified laws. *The Sentry's Lantern* concentrates on the evils of imperialism whereas *The Coffin* satirizes a bourgeois artist and his false world. *The Evening Lamp* also associates firmly with the playwright's social commitment. He depicts also the life of saints from contemporary point of view. The crisp dialogues and clear language are the significant features of Chattopadhayaya's plays. He shows little faith in the Western dramatic techniques. The models and techniques in his plays resemble Indian classical tradition.

The leading playwrights of this phase illuminate different aspects of social life in their plays. But constantly there is a negligible consideration of women's issues in their dramas. On the other hand, consideration for social issues of the minor playwrights of this phase is also noteworthy.

A.C. Krishnaswami's *The Two Twice Borns* (1914) deals with the issues like widow-marriage, the evil consequences of ill-assorted marriages between young girls and men. He strikes, in this way, the social evils in pre-Independence phase. S.M. Michael's *Nation Builders* deals with inter-caste as well as inter-sub-caste marriages among Hindus. V.V. Srinivasa Aiyangar's *Dramatic Divertisements*, a collection of playlets, exposes the angularities of the sophisticated middle-class people of Indian cities. Aiyangar shows an interest in dealing with the current social problems. Niranjan Pal's *The Goddess* (1924), a play in three acts, deals with corrupt priest craft and the exploitation of people in the name of religion. One more minor playwright of this phase, V. Narayanan, in his collection *Where God Is Not and Other Playlets* lashes at the corrupt priest craft as well the other social evils.

D.M. Borgaonkar's *Image Breakers* (1938) reveals the revolutionary attempts of Indian youth to change the norms of social institution, i.e. marriage. Balwant Gargi's *The Vultuer and Other Plays* is a collection of four playlets. The playwright shows his genuine faith to deal with the problems directly affecting our society. J.M. Lobo Prabhu's *Mother of New India* (1944) talks about one's personal love towards the cause of society. Ranganath, one more minor playwright of this phase deals with social evils like the professional dishonesty of doctors, corruption, jobbery and early marriages in his play *Milly* (1945). A.S.P. Ayyar's play *Sita's Choice* deals with the issue of widow marriages in the country.

These minor playwrights never followed any particular dramatic form. They were not either romantic or classicists in their approach. The contemporary relevance may not have judiciously taken into consideration by these playwrights. The prologue-epilogue technique and Sutradhara technique were directly or indirectly used by them. The dialogues in their plays were also not up to the mark. These plays partially represented the classical stage. The short plays were also written with a great deal of interest in this period. These plays received a modest attention of the audience. The playwrights chose social subjects for their short plays. It is really difficult to find any essence regarding woman's social as well as domestic life in their plays.

The study of pre-Independent male dramatic tradition brings to our notice that the issues of women were asided at large. Actually, Mahatma Gandhi inspired the participation of women in the freedom struggle of the nation but the status of woman was not attentively realized by the dramatists of this phase. Drama of any period can be an effective medium of social transformation. The human society can be presented in its true nature through drama. The playwrights, with a few exceptions, could not show their concern to present the issues of women. The women were not allowed to participate in the performances. They were not allowed even to spectacle the performances like men. Such restrictions might have forced the women writers of this time to maintain a considerable distance from writing as well as directing the plays. They remained largely reluctant to avail this art and tackle the issues related to their existence. The post-Independent phase connotes the similar fact.

VI

Asif Currimbhoy is the leading figure in the male tradition of post-Independence Indian English Drama because his plays delineate a perfect picture of post-Independent society. He handles the issue of vagabonds in his play *The Doldrummers*. His play *Thorns on a Canvas* deals with the lives and problems of artists whereas *The Miracle Seed* is a play about famine in Maharashtra. He published almost thirty plays in eighteen years of his dramatic career. The use of speeches in Currimbhoy's plays is as per the requirement of concerned play. He produced also some one-act plays. His one-act plays are noteworthy particularly for coherence in them.

The post-Independence Indian society confronted the conflict between the new and old concepts and customs to a great extent. With an implementation of Western educational system and imitation of the cultural traits, the new generation began to question the religious authority. Currimbhoy, in an authentic way, elaborates these issues in his plays.

The Indian English Drama in the earlier decades of this phase could not be as progressive as fiction and poetry. The lack of living theatre was the prominent cause behind it. Drama meant to be performed. If there is not any scope for performance; it is difficult for any writer to single out drama as his/her profession. The government even cared little the development of Indian English Drama. Hence, Indian English Drama could not excel up to the mark of expectations.

Tutun Mukherjee (2005: 10) has a pragmatic observation in the Preface to her seminal text *Staging Resistance*, regarding the state of post-Independence Indian drama:

> Post-Independence Indian drama has through the five decades grown more varied, rich, and diverse both in content and semiotics and draws upon myths, history, folklore, politics, society and quotidian life for material. Yet, in spite of its progress and contemporarization, there is one dimension of life's experiences that is still largely unexplored by Indian drama: women experiences.

Though the playwrights of this phase acquired a larger canvas for their dramatic expression; showed a marginal interest in representing the world of women.

The post-Independence Indian English Drama is crucial for the innovative techniques like mini plays and sustaining influence of Western theatre. The five-act plays of Elizabethan type attracted some playwrights of this phase. The use of prologue and epilogue pattern seems to be common during this dramatic phase. Pratap Sharma, one more prominent playwright of this phase, contributed this genre with his two plays—*The Professor has a Warcry* (1970) and *A Touch of Brightness* (1973). Both of the plays present the theme of sex in a different way. The political theme is blended here with the issue of sex. In *The Professor has a Warcry,* the dialogues are effective and there is an inclination for the present situation. On the other hand, *A Touch of Brightness* is typical mixture of garnish colours for Western audiences. One more playwright J.M. Leboprabhu's *Mother of New India* appeared before Independence. The volume of his plays *Collected Plays* contains six plays. The plays in the volume are: *Apes in Parlour*, *The Family Cage, Flages of the Heart, Winding Ways, Love Becomes Light* and *Dog's Ghost.*

The themes in Prabhu's plays substantially vary from one play to another. Exclusive melodramatic flavour to make a loss of naturality is the most significant feature of his plays. His plays are the best examples of his social conscience.

Nissim Ezekiel's *Three Plays* (1969) includes—*Nalini: A Comedy, Marriage Poem: A Tragi-Comedy* and *The Sleepwalkers: An Indo-American Farce*. The first two plays, i.e. *Nalini: A Comedy* and *Marriage Poem: A Tragi-Comedy* show contrast between the fake and the genuine. The third play in the sequence is a satire on an excessive fascination for American lifestyle.

Gurucharan Das's *Larins Sahib* (1970) is a historical play. The playwright fails to show separation of three avatars. G.V. Desani's *Hali* is an allegorical play. It presents a quest for fulfillment in life. The thematic richness and the style are highly appreciable here. Mr. Krishnamurti's *The Cloth of Gold* (1951), Sadashiv D. Rawat's poetic plays: *Immortal Song, The Killers* (1959), Pritish Nandi's *Rites for a Plebeian Stature* (1969) are some of the minor plays of this phase. Satya Dev Teggi's one-act plays *The Point of Light* and *End of Hunger* explore the different shades of social reality with the help of psychic modes of the characters. The woman in the plays of these male playwrights remains largely marginal. There is not any special consideration for her problems. She is stereotyped and expected to be loyal with her husband. These dramatists seldom emphasize the trauma of women in our conventional society.

VII

The Indian English Drama of twentieth century is a product of dramatic genius as such Mohan Rakesh, Girish Karnad, Badal Sircar and Vijay Tendulkar. They are the pioneers of 'The New Drama' in India. Mohan Rakesh contributed Indian English Drama with translation of his plays. He wrote the plays, viz. *Ashadh Ka Ek Din* (*One Day in Ashadah*), *Lehron ke Rajhans* (*The Great Swans of the Waves*), *Adhe Adhure* (*Half Way House*). The plays of Mohan Rakesh depict the mental conflict, helplessness, frustration, dissatisfaction and anger of the modern individuals. His plays are crucial for an appropriate presentation of modern Indian society. The modern individual in his plays is unable to adjust himself with the changing society. On the other hand, it is an individual's tragedy. His plays handle very carefully the man-woman relationship. His characters represent a set of ideology related to common life. His plays leave a great deal of impression on readers' mind for a skillful presentation. The woman in his play is bold and capable to take her personal decisions.

Badal Sircar has an ardent perception of the problems of middle-class Indian society. His existential attitude towards modern life is praiseworthy. Sircar's "Third Theatre" is a trend setter in various respects. According to Aparna Dharwadkar (2005: 70), it "...provides an alternative to both bourgeois urban realism and feudalistic rural forms."

Veena Dass (1990: 16) compliments Badal Sircar in following words: "If there is any playwright in the contemporary Bengali theatre who is capable of creating a genuine people's theatre, a theatre supported and created by the people and not merely performed by the people, it is Badal Sircar."

His plays, viz. *Bhooma*, *Procession* and *Stale News* are the best examples of this kind. The women characters are crucial in his plays because "Sircar creates a different space for women or different kind of women" (*ibid.*: 17). Sircar, to a greater extent, reforms the folk techniques in his performances.

Girish Karnad is among the leading playwrights in India. He wrote his first play in 1961. It was *Yayati*. The play was based on a story from *Mahabharata*. He would be remembered forever for his brilliant play *Tuglaq*. Here he attempts to correlate history with the contemporary situation. The play was published in the year 1964. His next play *Hayavadana* (1971) was based on Thomas Mann's short story *The Transposed Heads*. He is also known for his plays *Naga Mandala*, *The Fire and the Rain*, *Bali: The Sacrifice* and *The Dreams of Tipu Sultan*. The study of modern Indian drama now known as 'The New Drama' is incomplete without studying Girish Karnad's plays.

Vijay Tendulkar provides a political as well as social criticism through his plays. Like Mahesh Elkunchwar and Mahesh Dattani, he chooses realistic representations of contemporary urban social experience as the appropriate subject of his plays. The plays—

Silence! The Court is in Session, The Walls Between, I Won, I Lost, Vultures, Ghashiram Kotwal, Kamla, Sakharam Binder are the typical examples of this type. He is remarkable for creating new models through his plays. The woman in Tendulkar's plays is modern in thoughts and her actions. She is bold enough to decide the pattern of her personal life.

Mohan Rakesh, Badal Sircar, Girish Karnad and Vijay Tendulkar belong to the same generation of Indian playwrights. Their social experience, to a great extent, is similar but treatment is different. They were closely associated with the folk theatre of their respective region. To sum up, the playwrights "are busy in broadening the base of the Indian English drama in translation by introducing crisp dialogues and natural language, present-day problems and impressive craftsmanship in their plays without asking for their own cultural heritage".

The contemporary Indian English Drama receives a noteworthy contribution from Mahesh Dattani. It is really difficult to study contemporary Indian English Drama without mentioning his dramatic contribution. He is the first Indian English playwright to win the Sahitya Akademi Award for his play *Final Solutions and Other Plays* in the year 1998. The plays of Dattani probe deep into the Indian attitude towards communal differences, gender differences. Mahesh Dattani makes an abundant use of Indian mythology, rituals, traditions and contemporary problems India is beset with, but he elevates these themes to higher levels and touches the human chords that flow from love, happiness, sexual fulfillment and the problems of identity. He merges past and present and in this way his plays have a great contemporary value. The family unit is locale of Dattani's plays. Human relationships and the family unit have indeed been at the heart of his plays. *Tara* (1990) is about a boy and a girl who are joined together at the hip and have to be separated surgically, meaning death of one of two.

In *Dance Like a Man,* the man is excluded for his decision of choosing to dance like a woman, though his dancing is a way to express his identity. *Breavely Fought the Queen* (1991) questions the male and female role in the society. The playwright depicts here the plight of the helpless woman victims of male tyranny.

Seven Steps Around the Fire (1999) deals with the suppression of the marginalized 'Hijra' community. *Where There's a Will* (1988) presents the characters drawn from two generations, the father and the mother and their son and his wife, Preeti. The invisible and untouched issues lying in society are considered with priority by Dattani. His PLAYPEN, Performing Arts Group, Bangalore has been playing a crucial role in the development of drama. On the other hand, the women characters in Dattani's plays march a step ahead to dissociate themselves from the male-dominated structure. They have enough strength to stand with credence for their being as a woman. Uma in *Seven Steps around the Fire*, Lata in *Do the Needful*, Smitha in *Final Solutions*, Dolly, Alka and Lalita in *Bravely Fought the Queen,* Tara in *Tara* do not carry the load of patriarchy but strives for their survival after realizing their personal being. Mahesh Dattani presents, in this way, contemporary social realities considering woman's position, through his plays. In her tour de force, *Theatres of Independence,* Aparna Dharwadkar (2005: 69) observes: "Playwrights like Tendulkar, Elkunchwar, and Dattani who choose realist representations of contemporary urban social experience as the appropriate subject of drama and theatre." To conclude, the leading playwrights of this phase illustrate the social reality by giving an importance to women's issues as compared with the male playwrights of pre-Independence phase. The woman here is strong, straightforward and capable to face the difficulties in life. The representation of Indian woman in the contemporary male tradition in Indian English Drama differs widely from the earlier. It is more suggestive as far social reality is concerned.

VIII

The history of Indian English Drama estimates different factors behind man's central position in our society and shows how woman's image is being created in course of time. The art and literature have remained man-centred for centuries. The artists, philosophers and writers seldom tackled the issues of women. The women could obtain importance in social, political and educational spheres only after they got the right to vote. The women contributed for a national cause first time through Gandhi's non-cooperation movement. It may have such seeds of Indian feminism. The importance of women's participation was realized by Mahatma Gandhi. Therefore, he supported and encouraged the direct participation of women in his non-cooperation movement.

The issues of women in Indian English Drama were introduced in earlier period, to some extent, by the playwrights such as Sri Aurobindo and Rabindranath Tagore. But these masters of drama were contained to pose the image of woman as it was existed in earlier works. Though they staged the problems of Indian women, yet never put forth any revolutionary idea in this regard. Their observations were limited to social and cultural stature of Indian women. Hence, Tagore's Chitra never determines to perform any bold action. She is content to live with the limitations imposed on her by community. In *Chandalika,* Prakriti unfolds the similar tempo. She is very much restricted in the self-created circle. Her desire never goes beyond getting sexual pleasure. It seems as the playwrights like Tagore put them in the restrictions of self-zone, created generally under patriarchal impressions. The other playwrights for example, Sri Aurobindo, T.P. Kailasam and Chattopadhyaya share the equal experience in this regard.

The issues of women, to some extent, were taken to common folk for the very first time with the help of street theatre. The crucial advantage of street theatre is immediate and direct communication with general public. It is the easiest and effective medium to reach people. Safdar Hashmi's Jan Natya Manch played an important role in this connection. The playwright who modified these performances and expected a serious consideration for gender, political and created the women characters who were not capable enough to challenge the circle around social issues was Badal Sircar. He modified street theatre for better presentation of issues of women. "Street theatre had emerged as a strong medium for highlighting women's issues and an exclusive forum where women audiences could relate the issues" (Singh: 4). Long back, Raja Ram Mohan Roy's social movement was the earliest initiative taken in this regard. But for the centuries the voice of woman could not be heard. Indian English Drama could not be strong enough to proffer the issues of women. Most of the playwrights were indulged in presenting the stereotyped image of Indian woman. The woman was largely shown as a victim of social and political injustice. She was also shown as an unambitions, reluctant and ignorant regarding her own freedom. She was happy in her self-weaved nest. The woman, created by men in their plays is rather conventional hence subordinated.

IX

The female self receives a marginal representation in the plays of male writers in Indian English Drama. Except one or two plays, the woman character could not occupy the central position in the play. The issues of women are seldom discussed elaborately in these plays. On the other hand, the women playwrights, though less in number, attempt to stage the plight of Indian woman with a significant consideration. Under the impression of the classical theatre, they took most of the time the historical characters to depict the image of woman. The woman in their plays has certain limitations. She fails to express completely. Even though the attempt of women playwrights in making their women speak deserves to be mentioned, the women playwrights consider drama as a stratum to communicate the issues of women. But to a great extent, the women playwrights fail to create a gynotext based on gynocritics.

The socio-realism in most of the plays comes out with a complete notion of the ongoing transformation. Some of the playwrights before Independence of the nation could realize the importance of this art to make people aware of their exploitation under the British rule. Drama was not at all a new art for the Indian minds during this phase. They were well acquainted with it for a long time. In this way, it became an easier medium to interact with the masses. For the millions of illiterate Indians, inhabiting in remote villages, drama was a boon. Drama helped to fill up their minds with nationality.

On the other hand, the Western influence on these plays is not negligible. The Western techniques were followed in most of the plays. The native dramatic strategy also obtained a unified presentation in most of the plays of Indian soil. Social conscious of these playwrights is noteworthy but their apathy in introducing the issues of women should not be overlooked. The authentic woman's experience, therefore, lacks considerably in Indian English Drama.

It is difficult to recognize a genuine woman tradition in Indian English Drama. The women playwrights upto twentieth century could not cultivate substantially a world of real, authentic woman experience. Very few women playwrights in India could explore their real world through drama. But, on the other hand, the use of skillful dramatic devices in their plays deserves a special mention. The book attempts to explore the world of women's experience in the selected plays of Bharati Sarabhai, Mahasweta Devi and Manjula Padmanabhan because it is believed that these playwrights stand firmly before the dominant culture to voice the world of Indian women in their dramaturgy. Their plays demonstrate a world of woman that perceives different aspects of her life. Therefore, it is necessary to initiate a distinctive research to explore the woman's world in the plays of Indian women playwrights.

References

Bassnett, Susan (1984). "Towards a Theory of Feminist Theatre". In Schmid and Kestern, 445-58.

Bhatta, S.K. (1980). "Indo-English Women Playwrights." *Triveni*, 49(1) (April-June), 41-43.

_____ (1987). *Indian English Drama: A Critical Study*. New Delhi: Sterling Publishers Pvt. Ltd.

Dharwadkar, Aparna (2005). *Theatres of Independence*. New Delhi: Oxford University Press.

Dalmia, Vasudha (2006). *Poetics, Plays and Performances: The Politics of Modern Indian Theatre*. New Delhi: Oxford University Press.

Dass, Veena, Noble (1990). "Experiment and Innovation in Modern Indian Drama in Translation: The Plays of Mohan Rakesh, Badal Sircar, Vijay Tendulkar and Girish Karnad." In Pande and Taraporewala, 120-30.

Gupta, Balaram (1973). "A Note on Mrinalini Sarabhai's *The Captive Soil.*" *Essays on Indian Writing in English* (70-74). JIWE Publications.

Iyengar, Srinivas K.R. (1973). *History of Indian Writing in English.* Bombay: Sterling Pub. Pvt. Ltd.

Mukherjee, Tutun (2005). *Staging Resistance.* New Delhi: Oxford University Press.

Nagarwala, Arati (1969). *The Bait.* Calcutta: Writer's Workshop.

Pandey, Sudhakar and Taraporewala Freya (1990). *Contemporary Indian Drama.* Editors. New Delhi: Prestige Books.

Rangacharya, Adya (1971). *The Indian Theatre.* New Delhi: National Book Trust.

Schmid, Herta and Kestern, Aloysius, Van (1984). Editors. *Linguistic and Literary Studies.* Amsterdam and Philadelphia: John Benjamin Publishing Co.

Selden, Raman (1989). *A Reader's Guide to Contemporary Literary Theory*, Kentucky: University Press of Kentucky.

Showalter, Elaine. (1977). A *Literature of Their Own*: *British Women Novelists from Bronte to Lessing.* London: Virago.

_____ (1985). *The New Feminist Criticism: Essays on Women, Literature, and Theory.* New York: Pantheon.

_____ (1985). "Feminist Criticism in Wilderness". In Showalter, 243-71.

Singh, Anita (2009). "Aesthetic of Feminist Indian Theatre." *Roopkatha E-Journal.* 1:2 (Autumn). np.

Sharma, I.D. (2004). *Mahasweta Devi: Rudali—A Critical View.* Bareili: Prakash Book Depot.

Thakur, K.B. (1980). *Mother and Child. Triveni.* 2(2). (April-June): 123-64.

Tagore, Rabindranath. (1997). *Reminiscences,* London.

Weedon, Chris. (1987). *Feminist Practice & Poststructuralist Theory.* Cambridge MA & Oxford UK: Blackwell.

2

Women in Androcentric Society

> In the history of women's writing especially in the feminist critique 'gender' and 'genre' are frequently paired as coming from the same root.
>
> —Tutun Mukherjee

The base of the arguments in the present chapter is not restricted only to biological difference between men and women but to emphasize the social construction of gendered identities. At large, it attempts to illustrate process through which a woman is being constructed, restricted and isolated in phallocentric society. Hence, an attempt is made to illustrate gender-centred social reality to explore woman's state in male-centred world in the plays analyzed for the book. "Gender", de Lauretis argues, "is simply a system of generic classification: it places individuals within groups defined by a set of common characteristics. But gender is a strictly binary system" (Simion and Wallis: 78). It is believed that literature based on social reality binds together both the general and the particular situations. It emphasizes social as well as psychological reality. It foregrounds the different aspects playing a vital role in shaping literature with its base. The arguments made in the present chapter are formed, to some extent, by certain Marxist-Feminist principles to unearth the reality of woman's social condition as depicted in the selected plays of Bharati Sarabhai, Mahasweta Devi and Manjula Padmanabhan. Noted feminist critic, Helen Keysser

(1996: 5) argues: "Realism encourages us to forget the borders between stage and audience; the world of the play could easily be part of our world, and welcome to care about it almost as we would about our own life and communities." Marxist-feminist criticism is, therefore, apposite and excessively ideological as far socio-political stature of a woman is concerned. I quote Michele Barrett (1980: 09) to substantiate my argument.

"What then might be the object of Marxist feminism? In the most general terms it must be to identify the operation of gender relations as and where they may be distinct from, or connected with, the processes of production and reproduction understood separate and differentiate the inverted part by historical materialism. Thus it falls to Marxist feminism to explore the relation between the organization of sexuality, domestic production, the household and so on, and historical changes in the mode of production and systems of appropriation and exploitation." All the way, the core of argument here is the gender-based social reality focusing woman's position in phallocentric power structure.

Marxist-feminist literary study emphasizes that it is possible for women writers to speak the difference with the help of their sexuality. It focuses on the relation between reading and social realities. It combines at the same time, study of class with gender. To a great extent, it connects the personal with the real and also illustrates that the genital difference is not limited to gender difference only. But it helps indeed to make the study of women's writing more meaningful and broader. On the other hand, literature based on social reality binds the general and the particular situations to depict the interrelation between literature and society. It marches a step ahead to believe that the gender conflict is equated on the basis of class conflict. On the other hand, men writers do not bother to aside the issues of woman's social life in their literary works. Altogether, woman's social being remains nobody's concern. The interpretations believe here that there is no social reality outside the system of gender. To add further, Marxist-feminist criticism substantiates the aspect of woman's unexplored state in social life and provides a concrete base for expression. In this way, the gender-centred reality becomes pivotal for the study of the plays of these three playwrights.

I

Bharati Sarabhai has a dignified position as the only recognized Indian woman playwright during the pre-Independence phase of Indian English Drama. Her dramatic corpus, limited to two plays, depicts the diverse aspects of socio-political and cultural life of her time. Her women characters divulge the aspects of Indian womanhood with the help of self-realization and language. Writing, theatre, and education are the major areas of her interest. Bharati Sarabhai had an honour of becoming President of Ahmedabad Theatre Centre affiliated to Theatre Centre, India and ITI of UNESCO, respectively. She founded Nat Mandal, a drama academy and Art Theatre at Ahmedabad and became the first secretary. Bharati Sarabhai contributed for the leading journals such as *London Mercury*, *Art and Culture*, *New Horizon*, *The Modern Review*, *Modern English Poetry*, and *Partisan Review*. She participated as a volunteer in the Haripura Congress Civil Disobedience Movement between 1929 and 1939 with an interest in Gandhian ideals. She was jailed for three months during 1942 Quit India Movement.

Bharati Sarabhai's first English play *The Well of the People* (1942) won praise from the literary stalwarts such as T.S. Eliot, E.M. Forster, Rabindranath Tagore, etc. The play is eulogized in Dr. M.K. Naik, and S. Mokashi Punekar edited anthology *Perspectives on Indian Drama* under the chapter "The Plays of Bharati Sarabhai." Her other play *Two Women* (1952), an Indian social drama, was produced at the Excelsior Theatre, Mumbai by Hima Kesarkodi and at the Kenya National Theatre, Nairobi by Nalini Devi and Appa Pant in February 1952 and December 1952, respectively. The play was also performed at the Wayne State University School of Drama, U.S.A. Her two Gujarati plays—*Be Nari* and *Ghar Lakhoti* were published by Gurjar Grantha Ratna, Ahmedabad. Her plays produced an electrifying effect in the process of involvement of women writers in dramaturgy.

The play *The Well of the People* is a result of Bharati Sarabhai's active participation in the national freedom struggle. It gave her an opportunity to experience the socio-political and economical dimensions of Indian life. Bharati Sarabhai's long stay in Sabarmati Ashram brought her ideologically close to Gandhi's philosophy of social realism. Secondly, she acted as a volunteer under Nehru's command at the Haripura Session of Congress. But the real inspiration behind the play was her visit to Kumbha Mela at Haridwar in April 1938, and the story appeared in the *Harijan*. It was a true story of an aged and destitute Brahmin woman in a remote village of Bihar. She has a long-cherished dream to visit Benaras, the shrine, at least once in her lifetime. She is set, all the way to spend her hard-owned money for the pilgrimage. But the newly aroused Gandhian spiritual idealism captivates her to the extent of taking the decision of constructing a well for the *Harijans* (untouchables) in her village.

The playwright discloses the aspects of the play in her preface to it. According to her, the form of the play is

> "...players in a drama, but is actually the static representation in one moment of the time of different characters fixed in their different environments with a changeless background behind..."(2). The playwright thus achieves a respective position with an instigation of a new form to Indian Street Theatre. The protagonist of the play, an aged woman, is an inarticulate in the play. She represents 'dumb millions' because she speaks quite a few bearable sentences in the play.

The social endeavour, offered to the old woman in Gandhian pattern of spiritual idealism, challenges her conventional religious faith but fails to cut down the roots, completely. Actually, Gandhian idealism itself strived more to give a rational form to ancient spiritualism. Bharati Sarabhai reveals the old woman's transformation simultaneously with the social condition in rural India and its relation with newly emerged Gandhian leadership on Indian horizon. Mahatma Gandhi began his freedom movement only after visiting Indian villages. The rural India was the real India for him. Sarabhai's fascination for Gandhism helps indeed to develop the play as an archetype of Indian womanhood before

Independence and socio-political as well as economic condition of farmers and peasants, on the other hand. In this way, it is an archetype of subalterns such as peasants, workers and women.

One of the crucial plays in the Indian women's dramaturgy, *The Well of the People*, is an emblem of Gandhian philosophy of socio-realism depicting the state of Indian womanhood. Claude Levi Strauss (1967: 52), a celebrated Marxist anthropologist, suggests: "A mythical character marches on the Hegelian logic of thesis, antithesis, and synthesis" (52). Gandhian myth, similarly, has an essence in Indian literature. His character is mythical as far his stature in the midst of the issues of subordinate communities is concerned.

Based on a story, appeared in *Harijan*, the play depicts an old woman's innermost passion to visit Haridwar for the salvation of her dead husband and son. Despite economical constrains, she keeps her dream alive by working hard for small wages. She accumulates some amount and visualizes her trip in near future. But her growing concern in Gandhian ideology of unto this last shifts her conventional religious faith. She decides lastly to build a well for Harijans in her village and vicinity. But she could not see the well built as she dies of old age.

The play opens with 'a scene of fantasy'. It opens with the formation of two different groups on different parts of the stage. The playwright follows street theatre characteristics to imply community participation throughout the play. Hence, participation of the peasants in performance becomes noteworthy. Gargi Balwant (1962: 173) puts on record: "People and players, the two pillars of theatre kept apart for so long, joined and became one whole." Bharati Sarabhai develops the play with a clever use of chorus. It helps indeed to impart an individual's sensitiveness to a spiritual situation. To state further, Greek chorus, known as classical chorus has a sustaining impression on Eliot's play *Murder in the Cathedral*. Bharati Sarabhai has done a crafty rendering from Eliot's play in this regard. The poetic form of dialogue, to some extent, restores the Western conception of Poetic Drama in Eastern context but copes up well with Popular Theatre in India. We are at Haridwar scene where thousands of devotees are ardent to fulfill their indominatable desire of taking a deep in the Ganges. The passion of devotees can be compared with a river's earnest desire to meet the sea. The woman chorus at Haridwar communicates the presence of women for Kumbha Mela in following words:

> ...have sat on the road in absent mood, caught like pitchers down-naked emptying emptying their breasts to sons velvet-waisted.... (11)

The whole Haridwar scene is a microcosmic picture of India. The Kumbha Mela has a spellbound working on spiritual Hindu minds. The men and women believe that their life is incomplete without pilgrimage on this holy occasion. But the life is not going to change just by pilgrimage to these sacred places. By visiting these places, one cannot release himself or herself from earthly responsibilities. The Gandhian worker, Chetan, emphasizes this fact and adds further that the people in our country are no doubt religious but they are certainly careless towards worldly responsibilities. For Hindus, pilgrimage to sanctified places like Haridwar, Kashi is headway to salvation. "For the Indians faith means grouping towards the utter formless God through the vestiges of different godheads who may be identified with the different aspects of nature" (Nandakumar: 186). The conventional Indians have been showing their faith in pilgrimage century after centuries. But Gandhi's spiritual idealism, for the very first time, enables these conventional minds to change their way.

The playwright skillfully shifts now to a village scene. There is not any conventional division like acts and scenes in the play. Hence, the movements on stage and also the dialogues help for outward transformation. The playwright uses background for this purpose. The group formed by Gandhian workers deals with the life of old woman. The spatial dynamics among the different scenes helps to explore the facets of social reality.

The playwright presents a realistic and emotive picture of rural India before Independence. The Indian villages were destroyed by the masters and the millions of trained artisans and craftsmen, spinners, weavers, potters, tanners, smelters and smiths crowded themselves into agriculture. In this way, there was a shift from being a country of combined agriculture and manufacture to an agriculture colony of the Britishers. The manufacturers and farmers were compelled to pay heavy duty on their goods. Gandhiji, in the midst of British tyranny, appeared as the leader of the nation. Sehagal (1967: 6) in Bhattacharya's *A Goddess Named Gold* observes: "Gandhiji touched our spirit as if slept. Wakened, we became the equals of our men folks. Proud, chins up, we marched in a column of our own...." It was the time to come together and emancipate these people from the present state of gloom and despair. Gandhiji, as a crusade against social evils in Indian society, emphasized the need of collective efforts in this regard. The volunteers like Chetan were doing their level best to prepare the people for Gandhi's mission. They had faith in a cardinal dictum 'better to light one candle than to curse the darkness'. As a visionary, Gandhi insisted for the fundamental changes in the rural parts of the country. Before the Independence, the task assigned to Gandhian workers was to orient rural Indians for the freedom.

The pragmatic attitude of young Gandhian workers like Chetan finds no change in the day-to-day living of the common people even after a long pilgrimage to holy places. His mind is unable to comprehend the fact, i.e. fascination of Hindus for sacred places.

The young Indians strive to interrogate the conventional spiritualism only after advent of Gandhism. Gandhi was ruling over the sense and sensibility of common Indians.

B.A. Pathan's (1984: 11) observation in this regard is worth quotable:

> ...Mohandas Gandhi was a biological phenomenon in human form, but Mahatma Gandhi who was the very embodiment of Truth, Non-violence and other noble qualities, who swayed the Indian heart and mind for many years reminding one of the Gita's saying *Sabhawami Yuge Yuge.*

The chorus standing opposite to Gandhian workers captivates readers' attention for a beautiful narration of Haridwar scene. The rising of full moon magnifies the charm and on the other hand, Sarabhai's poetic excellence reaches pinnacle with a strong, distinctive and authentic voice. The voice epitomizes suppressed inner self of an old woman who chooses the new path for her life. Robert Frost's paradigm of the road not taken is contextual here. One has an inner self which seldom ventures to stop crawling on conventional or forced thought. The old woman's inner voice grills:

> Why do you go to Haridwar, to Kashi Varanasi, O my soul, when I am within?
>
> Pilgrim, pilgrim why, what is it you seek outside? (22)

The God is within. He is an Omnipotent. The presence of God can be experienced by one's deeds. The great saint Kabir has also stated rightly this metaphysics in his famous *dohas* (a versical composition), popularly known as *Kabirwani.* The social distinction of Indian society before Independence was characterized mainly on the basis of the issue of domination. Therefore, the subalterns in Indian society eagerly waited for a crusader to lift them from the severe pangs of life. The Marxist axiom also directs at class-conflict as a root cause of social imbalance. Bharati Sarabhai succeeds in *The Well of the People* to portrait the reality of social imbalance in pre-independent Indian society. The farmers and peasants were exploited by the Britishers and also by the usurers. It was an initial phase of Sahukar raj in India. In the midst of an episode of indolence, they were fortunate to have Gandhian workers like Chetan with a humane concern for their problems. They were working in Indian villages to spread the Gandhian message among the villagers. They were sharing the sorrow and consoling these poor people for ill-treatment they have been receiving for a long time.

It was a Herculian task for Gandhian workers to challenge the conventional spiritualism. The peasants, farmers, and other working-class communities in Indian villages had an innermost faith in conventional spiritualism determined by the earlier generations. The task of these workers is represented here with their attempt to transform old woman's faith. Why the conventional mind was to be challenged? Probably, to replace the previous one with rationality. The Gandhian workers had been toiling to cultivate the minds of these villagers to encash the crop of rationalism. It was also an attempt to make them sensible of their pathetic state under British governance. The magical leadership of Gandhi helped them to stay united, fight for their fundamental rights and lead towards a complete freedom. The transformation begins with the influencing words of these Gandhian workers.

The peasants expressed their innermost pleasure for the transformation taking place around because for the very first time, someone bothered seriously their way of living. Gandhi initiated a mission to change the lives of these people. He charged strongly the oppression of workers, peasants and women under British rule. Dr. Radhakrishnan (2008: 11) resonates Gandhi's undefiled concern for poor people in following words:

> ...we have millions of people who are the victims of poverty, who are under-nourished and under-housed, whose lives are an unceasing struggle from youth to the old age, until at last death comes to their rescue and still their aching hearts. These conditions are not due to pitiless nature, but to the inhuman system which cries out to be abolished, not in the interest of India but of the whole humanity.

Mahatma Gandhi's broadcast address from London to America in 1931 highlighted his growing displeasure for the condition of Indian villages under the British rule. Mahatma Gandhi's stand was crystal clear. He emphasized: "a responsible agrarian population and the stable, level-headed people of small-agricultural market-towns must dominate the cultural, social, economic and noble objects" (*ibid.*: 14).

The work of Mahatma Gandhi was carried out particularly by the ardent workers was the only sublime way to introduce 'the dimension of change' in the lives of millions of farmers and peasants in Indian villages. They were committed to kindle at least a flicker of new knowledge in the minds of these poor people.

The spinning wheel was very important for these workers. It was 'an instrument to abolish the economical slavery' to reach the destination of economical independence. Gandhi's revolution methods generally commenced at micro level but possessed all the essential qualities. The method to work for these poor Indians was not conventional. He worked in a different way and also believed in doing something worthwhile for the upliftment of these people. Gandhi called them Harijans—the sons of God. He found the presence of God in them. Gandhiji imparted ability in these workers that they became enough confident to proclaim:

> We said pilgrim, pilgrim of this Late time,
> Drink, drink from dreaming soul of Rebel Gandhi. (29)

The playwright explores here a mediocre position of a pathetic woman. The old woman, though being the leading character in the play, speaks a few bare sentences throughout the play. She represents in this way 'dumb millions'. The phrase 'dumb millions' represents the oppressed state of millions of Indian women who had not any say in the issues related to power structure. Her entry on the stage is casual. A chorus of women notices her appearance. She has not been provided enough space to occupy any position on the stage. In this way, she dangles on the stage. The old woman carries for years the burden of pilgrimage. The burden is nothing but an imposition on a woman's mind in an androcentric culture. She is not encouraged for an impregnable ideological stand. Therefore, a woman in Indian society depends on men for various reasons. Old woman decides to visit Haridwar and Kashi out of the patriarchal pressure. She has to follow the phallocentric norms imposed on her life. A woman ought to seek salvation of male members of her family and obtain status of an ideal woman. In this way, her burden is more psychological than physical. The old woman remarks: "I could not go. All I have is not enough" (30). She represents the faith of thousands of Hindu women like her who find completion of life only in terms of their pilgrimage to sacred places like Kashi and Haridwar. In this way, her indomitable faith in pilgrimage is of representative kind. She believes strongly that pilgrimage only can open the gate of salvation for women like her. The Gandhian workers Chetan and Vichitra talk simultaneously about Haridwar and old woman. It is really difficult for these young workers to believe that the Hindus are unable to go beyond their innermost desire for pilgrimage. They focus on the need of old woman's religious transformation because Gandhi always supported the cause of women's empowerment. He believed firmly that a woman can make the change possible.

The old woman keeps alive her dream of pilgrimage. The village scene where the peasants have already formed a group, mocks at old woman's deep-longing for pilgrimage. It is, as they consider, beyond old woman's capacity at this stage of her life. She will not be in position to fulfill her desire due to old age. On the other hand, the hatred of fellow workers is symbolic. It represents the conventional battle between old and new ideals. A conventional mind finds it difficult to adjust with new. On the other hand, when a woman is the cause of change, it becomes more difficult to accept it. The chorus of peasants talks about the old woman.

We have seen, seen her at weaving shed, Come late at end of each long day and stand, Upon twilight that winds her cowdust through The scattering basket of sunset harvest. (33)

The old woman, a Maithili Brahmin, was forced to marry at an immature stage of her life with an old man. The story of old woman raises, to some extent, predicament of widows in Indian society. Noted writer and activist Mahasweta Devi has perfectly illustrated an old woman, Sanichari's fray for survival in her short-story *Rudali*. Likewise, the old woman in the play is unable to rest with peace even at this difficult stage of her life. There are a great number of widows in our country, forced to toil even after becoming old hence dependent.

Old woman lives with a dream of Haridwar pilgrimage. One comes across now a beautiful narration in this part of the play. The accumulated coins for pilgrimage to Benaras seem like piled stones and bricks. The stone and brick symbol helps to percept that it is preparation of the road to walk and reach her destination.

Salvation to the dead soul of her husband and son is found in pilgrimage to Benaras. Her biological being as a woman cripples on phallocentric traits because she finds personal salvation in the dead souls of her son and husband. The other aspect of her psychic state is also noteworthy because it is beginning of a transformation. Her conventional faith wanes after newly-awakened socio-spiritual idealism of Mahatma Gandhi. The transformation of the old woman is symbolic. It shows a growing concern of upper-class women for the lives of lower class people. Gandhi expected the commitment of women of this class particularly to change the life of these pathetic people. It is a kind of alienation because alienation needs not to be a physical condition always. It can be a psychological transmutation also. Her shadow falls equally on both the sides of the ground. As stated earlier, the two sides of the stage symbolize state of her mind through two groups of chorus. The falling of her shadow on both the sides denotes a change. It is her inability to single out between a trip to Benaras and her social responsibility. The advent of Gandhian socio-religious idealism never challenged anybody's conventional religious faith but inspired for a rational rumination. With changing time, Gandhi urged strongly for transformation at the level of one's thinking. Gandhi stated somewhere "when it is time for social transformation, women should lead the line". This message of socio-spiritualism is carried out further, with a greater effect in Indian villages by the devoted workers like Sanatan and Vichitra. They never expected any new kind of idealism but helped the conventional people like old woman for broad thinking. But the next group of chorus on the stage insists old woman to keep her going on conventional track with her personal dream. For them, it is not necessary to choose any new principle. They were surprised to see old woman is set all the way to change her mind.

Gandhi's message of change appeals old woman's mind. It never appeals alike to the conventional minds of other workers and peasants. Old woman's decision to build a temple-well for her villagers is a result of an air of change. The old woman realizes that it is difficult for her to build a temple-well out of the money she saved for her pilgrimage. Therefore, she decides to offer herself as a slave to the moneylender for getting more money for this noble cause. Her decision to build the well, in this way, is spontaneous and not a compulsion. Sanatan and Vichitra doubt initially but old woman's resolution:

> If I can build a well beside the temple Before I die, people who pray may drink At my well. People in the evening bells And more and more good folk from far will come
>
> And at our earthen mother's breast repose
>
> And resting pray, blessing god for his cool wells. (41)

challenges their distrust. The Gandhian workers Chetan and Vichitra echo the similar impression of Gandhi on old woman's mind. She inspires them but realizes that very few days remained to fulfill her innate wish of building a temple-well. Old woman falls straight on the ground. She dies but leaves behind the message of newly awakened socio-spiritual idealism. It is, all the way, meaningful whatever she did for the peasants of her village. She adds a dimension to the Gandhian mission by realizing herself and also letting others to realize it. Basically, in the last days of her life, she lives a complete life. The playwright merges the village scene with Haridwar scene at the end to create a different impression. To conclude, the play explores a woman's stature in phallocentric society. As Marxist-Feminism raises the gender-based issues by challenging the power structure, likewise Bharati Sarabhai attempts here the issues related to woman's subordination to tackle the status of Indian women of pre-independent society and to the end, directs millions of women towards the social change.

The patriarchal society expects a woman to be more honest in performing her responsibilities as a wife or a mother than a woman. It means old woman has her presence in the play more according to phallocentric codification. She is not expected to believe or follow her dreams. She ought to keep in mind her responsibility and spend her remaining life for it. The restrictions imposed on her by the power structure do not accept her personal right to decide what she should do after her husband's death. Gender-centric connotation demands a woman's consideration in terms of her being as a woman and not the different roles labeled. Hence, what is more interesting to the end of the play from gender-centric point of view is not old woman's failure in building a well for untouchables but her courage in going against the power system and taking the decision of her choice at any cost. It is a kind of liberation on her part because it helps her to listen the inner call and act accordingly.

The other play of Bharati Sarabhai, *Two Women* (1952) is an example of different aspects of Indian womanhood. The title of the play *Two Women* is suggestive in various respects as it deals with different life attitudes and the state of Indian womanhood. The playwright explores social realism through the life of two women—Anuradha and Urvashi. The spatial essence of the play assists to discover the different aspects of social reality. Anuradha represents a typical Indian woman who cares more for her responsibilities as a mother and a wife. On the other hand, Urvashi, her friend dissociates herself quite easily from worldly responsibilities. She is, in other words, an unexpressed, unheard Anuradha, urging for isolation from conventional life after being a perfect housewife. For Anuradha, visit to Himalaya is the only way to ensure the long-cherished salvation dream. Urvashi does not give up the conventional Hinduism but does not think like a conventional woman. In her personality, there is a perfect combination of old and new. She is able to take decisions of her own and also to stick up them. It is not like conventional Hindu spiritualism where salvation is sought at the latter stage of life. Urvashi, a middle-aged woman, seeks it quite earlier in her life. In this way, being a liberated woman, she meets her subjectivity and language unlike her mate Anuradha who finds it difficult to obtain her subjectivity.

Bharati Sarabhai stages the world of two dancer-friends—Anuradha and Urvashi in *Two Women* which leads ultimately to explore different facets of Indian womanhood. Anuradha, a woman with the stature of a queen spends her life like a typical woman and identified particularly as Kanak Raya's wife. Kanak Raya, her husband prefers peculiar Western lifestyle. He does not like Anuradha's conventional Indianized way of living and also her inclination for rituals. He expects that she should accept his lifestyle. Their daughter, Lata, like her mother, takes interest in classical dance and prefers her mother's way of living. Therefore, Kanak appoints Miss Boulten, a foreign tutor to teach Western etiquettes to Lata.

The palace of Kanak Raya experiences some changes with Urvashi Devi's arrival. A battle between two cultures begins and in this way, Anuradha receives an opportunity for self-realization. She decides to become a *jogen*, like Urvashi and to spend the remaining life in Himalaya. Lata also shows interest in following her mother's footsteps. On the other hand, Miss Boulten, Sudha, Darshan and Kanak dislike Anuradha's decision prior to their personal views. To the end, Anuradha cancels her visit to Himalaya to look after her ill husband. In this way, the playwright illustrates here how a woman compromises with self, subjectivity and language in a male-dominated society.

The entire play takes place in the sitting room of Kanak Raya. The play opens with a frank conversation between Anuradha and her brother Darshan. The dialogue between them is an account of their childhood memories, a deep-longing for those blessed days. Anuradha, after eighteen years of her marriage is not happy with her position in the house. Anuradha is a typical Indian housewife who cares more for the family values. Hence, she prefers to remain silent during these eighteen years of her married life. It suggests more a cultural distinction. She does not challenge the male-centred rule in the home. The playwright maintains purposely a distinction between two parts of the living room. Kanak Raya's part has a Western outlook. Anuradha's part, on the other hand, is a typical Indian side. Darshan gifts a portrayal of Himalaya to Anuradha. Darshan has not any inclination for this place but Anuradha considers it as the only way to attend salvation. The transformation or shift in the faith is not easily possible. The last eighteen years of marriage failed to build Anuradha's level of confidence as an independent woman. She has been left incomplete and lives completely under her husband's control. Kanak Raya, her husband, the minister of state, feels more relaxed in Western attires. He has faith in Western culture and takes pleasure in following the Western lifestyle. He feels that Anuradha should follow his lifestyle. He comes to know about Urvashi Devi's arrival. It is interesting to know what he thinks about her arrival.

> ANURADHA : Urvashi Devi is coming here, later in the evening.

> She asked Lata to sing to her today. We shall hear what she thinks about Lata's singing.
>
> KANAK : Oh, because Urvashi Devi is coming!
>
> Well, well we find it difficult to recall such an exciting event in the last few years.
>
> I can't remember such trepidation over any other guest.
>
> Not even when the Viceroy came! Extraordinary. (13)

Kanak Raya is keen to teach Western etiquettes to Lata, his daughter. Therefore, he appoints Miss Boulten, a young British teacher, to serve the purpose. He says: "Not that I have anything against your patronizing home made products. Quite good in their own way, but don't go so far as to patronize home-made ideas" (15). The endless discussions with the news of Urvashi Devi's arrival are quite interesting, in their own way. One of the feminist principles denotes women's natural tendency in showing an interest in trivial discussions. Similarly, women in Kanak Raya's home keep themselves busy in sense and non-sense discussions.

The news of Urvash Devi's arrival is celebrated as a festive occasion in the home. The way Urvashi Devi interacts with the family members of Anuradha signifies her mature sense. Before her arrival, there was an unending suspicion about her character. But afterwards a simple and natural behaviour of Urvashi Devi pleases everyone in the home. In Freudian terminology, *repression* is a storehouse of all unfulfilled desires or traumatic past events and experiences. This storehouse of traces has a strong influence on all human actions. When sublimated, the repressed feelings become 'noble' or great. The repression of genuine feelings takes Urvashi's personality to the highest stature. She owns a massive group of followers to her credit. They respect her sacrifice and sanguinity. Though, being of middle age, she has not any desire and urge of material gains. She believes whole-heartedly in following the path of isolation. She has an utmost passion to stay in the Himalayin mountains for the rest of her life. Her longing for Himalaya is different than old woman's longing for Benaras in *The Well of the People*. The old woman in the play desires for the pilgrimage only during the last stage of her life. It is one of the ashrama's in Hinduism, i.e. *Sanyashram*. Urvashi Devi is rather leading *Wanprasthashram*, a bit difficult stage to follow for an individual. Urvashi Devi's personality shows a relation with one of the feminist traits denoting capacity to take personal decisions, irrespective of social taboo. She is one who denies the beaten track to trudge.

The influence of Mirabai on Urvashi's personality cannot be dissociated easily. Like her, Urvashi gives up the worldly pleasures in pursuit of God's company. She became a *jogen* to ascertain the sublime pleasures of life. The upper and middle class women of late fifties and sixties in certain Indian families were occupied with a divine concern to leave the worldly worries behind to seek the perpetual solace. Anuradha's longing for the Himalaya intends the similar purpose whereas Urvashi's dissociation from the life after becoming a child widow shows her strong inclination for consolation. She cares her personal feelings as she denies to spend the remaining life in patriarchal bondage. As mentioned earlier, Bharati Sarabhai does not present these two women as individuals but representatives of Indian womanhood with contrasting attitudes. Anuradha undergoes a conflict of making a choice. She has to follow either her intimate friend or to stay at home to continue her family responsibilities. She is obliged to look after her sick husband. This is where she has a difficulty in taking personal decision. Urvashi Devi is not in such confusion because her decision to remain unmarried shows her ability and desire to swim against the stream. Hence, her character is crucial for her inward capacity to choose the track which is hardly possible for others to follow. The playwright portrays, in this way, the human tendency. As psychological study states, human mind reckons more on the environment in which he/she has been brought up. Urvashi Devi's father almost supports her decision of segregation. Her father's support to her decision states plainly the type of atmosphere in which she is brought up. On the other hand, Anuradha is groomed in a different atmosphere. She was rather prepared to follow her responsibilities faithfully. She keeps herself constantly in a squabble between the choice of what her mind suggests and heart urges. She fails to deny any of them, completely. Her conflict, likewise Shaw's protagonist in the play *Candida*, creates difficulties in making a choice between compulsion of mind and response of heart. Radical Feminism asserts that change for an individual does not occur without a moral transformation. Women have been generally prepared in such a way that they are compelled to follow male-constructed morals as a social morality. In course of time, the patriarchal moral becomes a code of conduct. Anuradha accepts the male-centred moral and lives her life, accordingly. She does not bother to follow them because she takes this moral as her personal responsibility in androcentric structure. But after her friend Urvashi's arrival, she dares to transform her faith and in real sense accepts the change.

The other members of the family are busy in futile discussions on Urvashi Devi's arrival. Miss Boulton interacts with Darshan and Sudha. The subject of their discussion never goes beyond Urvashi Devi's arrival. Men and women in general fail to accept a woman superior to them. Sudha dislikes unending talks on Urvashi Devi. Sudha, niece of Kanak Raya, is quite aggressive in her temperament. It is quite appropriate to her immature age and incomplete perceptions of life. Darshan, on the other hand, thinks in a different way. He is pragmatic and has a different type of affection for Urvashi Devi.

Kanak and Miss Boulton see at Urvashi Devi from the Western point of view. Kanak finds it uneasy to accept Anuradha's growing concern and appreciation for Urvashi. On the other hand, Miss Boulton finds it difficult to accept the impression Urvashi Devi has created on the minds of her followers. Urvashi Devi, a spiritual woman, devoted to Krishna *bhakti* (devotion) getting more and more followers and that is well in the modern world, surprises Miss Boulton. Anuradha, in her discussion with Urvashi is interested to explain her future plan. She is keen about her visit to Himalaya. For the first time, a change is observed in her disposition. Lata, Anuradha and Kanak Raya's daughter is now under Urvashi Devi's influence. She decides to accompany her mother along with Urvashi Devi to Himalayan abode. The playwright deals with Sudha's radical and straightforward opinion. Besides, Miss Boulton's balanced observation, Shastri's (Urvash Devi's father) argument, Darshan's acceptance of having no interest in Sudha and Kanak Raya's anxiousness for his wife. The playwright is concerned here to unearth the dynamics of social reality through relational pattern among the characters and their actions as well reactions and also a gender perspective.

Sudha's outrageous anger and jealous for Urvashi Devi is the result of Darshan's lack of interest in her after Urvashi's arrival. She accepts her presence in the home with great difficulty. Darshan is not ready to accept Kanak Raya's condition of marrying Sudha for the economical assistance to complete his higher education because he finds: "Sudha is not my idea of India" (16). She shows a number of signs of immaturity in her personality. She mentions: "...Aunty has got hold of a bogus Swami. The usual holy claptrap to entice women away. The danger is uncle doesn't believe that his wife can really leave him, ever" (61).

Change in the relationship between Anuradha and Kanak Raya astonishes Sudha. On the other hand, she feels insulted for the change in Darshan's behaviour. Darshan does not consider her now either a perfect Indian or convent product but a half-breed of both. Her dream of marriage with Darshan is like building a castle in the air. Sudha's immaturity, incomplete comprehension, and growing jealous for Urvashi Devi kept her restricted in her ideas. If one considers it just a fault of her age then there is not justice with Lata. Though she is of Sudha's age, approximately, shows rare signs of immaturity. She is more mature than her actual age. Her fascination for a disinterested life shows clearly her prepared mind. Miss Boulton scolds Sudha for her unfit traits whereas Sudha blaims Urvashi for the change in the house.

Anuradha's decision to leave for Himalaya is consequence of Urvashi Devi's arrival. Kanak is unable to convey any decision or stop his wife and daughter from their trip to Himalaya. On the other hand, Sudha's subconscious mind plays contrasting roles. She evinces herself as dear niece of Kanak Raya and depicts anger and jealous for Urvashi Devi.

Urvashi Devi's father unearths one more aspect of human behaviour in the play. His love and concern for Urvashi comes out of fame she has been accumulating for her father. He is not interested like any other father to get her daughter re-married. Point to be argued that he has faith in "A woman's place is by her husband. This is an argument to which there is no reply" (65). His conventional mind does not allow him to take any off-beat decision. Sudha's dislike for both Shastri and his daughter Urvashi continues to affect her language. The Freudian term *Repression* denotes one's unadmitted, unexpressed desire. There lies a dominant desire on Sudha's part to captivate Darshan and be forever of him. Urvashi's untimely and unwanted arrival vanishes Sudha's dream. It forces her to be in the camp of her haters. Her behaviour, in this way, is more psychologically controlled than socially formed.

There is a lasting impression of the dialogue between Kanak and Shastri. Both of them, to a great extent, have been voyaging in the same boat. Shastri laments demise of his wife and hollowness after it. There is a sense of incompleteness and meaninglessness. He speaks: "My eyes did not see, after she died. They do not see to this day, nor can they close in rest" (65). Kanak Raya's dejection is somehow different. He realizes now the need of Anuradha's company at this stage of his life. The playwright, to state clearly, depicts Kanak Raya's psychic state through Shastri's emptiness. The playwright does not think like radical feminists who disregard men in the lives of women at any stage of life. Miss Boulton's observation throughout the play associates closely with writer's following in her writing career.

Kanak Raya experiences a change in his attitude. He does not hesitate to admit Anuradha's importance in his life for the first time. The relationship of any kind necessities time and maturity both. Husband-wife relationship is no way an exception to this realization. Mahatma Gandhi's observation in this regard is worth quotable. He mentions:

> I admit that between husband and wife there should be no secrets from one other. I have a very high opinion of the marriage tie. I hold that husband and wife merge in each other. They are one in two or two in one. But these things cannot be regulated mechanically. (Gandhi: 65)

Kanak Raya admits further: "Miss Boulton, do you know that I have not spent one day away from my wife except when I had to. I can't relax when she is not here" (70).

Anuradha never considers her plan as an escape from her responsibilities but feels: "...on the lap of Himalaya, at the breast of mother Ganga, alone with the voices of meditation.... No timepiece—only the sun and moon to remind one" (71). Meditation and hope for a complete new life helped Anuradha to proceed in the direction of Himalaya. Urvashi gave her an opportunity to discover 'self'. Both of the women stand distinctly in their approach towards life. One is little careful about the life responsibilities in life whereas the other has already completed them without any failing or otherwise. It comes out as a consequence of their realization of life. But "Realization cannot occur in epicurean perversion or an ascetic denial of life" (Nandakumar: 194).

Anuradha's conversation with Guruji reveals certain facts of her married life before him. Anuradha's belief: "My life does not seem mine any more! Slipping away from my very hands; pouring out every moment, pouring into the sand with his life-line!" (78) focuses on Anuradha's genuine perturb for husband's health.

Kanak Raya insists Anuradha to accompany him to Ceylon trip. Anuradha is not at all interested to accompany him. The ideological conflict between Kanak Raya and Anuradha as the followers of Western and oriental culture occupies a great deal of importance in the play. Anuradha, like Urvashi, is an ardent follower of Mirabai. The *bhajans* of Mira have a prominent place in her day-to-day life. The *Prem Bhakti Bhajans* of Mirabai occupy a cardinal place in the play. Saint Mira's concept of divine love brought a sea-saw change in the *bhakti* tradition. Anuradha's decision to stay at Himalayan hermitage is a consequence of self-realization. Mirabai, five centuries earlier, left the palace and gave up the stature of a queen and became *jogen* of Lord Krishna. Anuradha, like Mira, feels that the path of salvation leads one to sacrifice the physical pleasures and move to Himalaya. There are four *yogas* or ways as suggested in Hinduism. Out of these four, *Bhaktiyoga* is considered next to *Karmayoga*. It expects total surrender to the God, the Almighty. Mirabai was a true

Karmayogi because she had followed with faith the path of an unattached, unmotivated actions and thoughts and then only became a *Bhaktiyogin*. To put in nutshell, the path of *Bhaktiyoga* assimilates with the path of *Karmayoga* and it is not possible to differentiate both from each other. Anuradha is not a true *Karmayogin* like Mira because her life is incorporated with motivated and attached actions like any other ordinary woman's life. It is only after Urvashi Devi's arrival, she determines to leave the palace in search of God. Conventionally speaking, *Bhaktiyoga* is impossible without *Karmayoga*. Hence, Anuradha's passion for *Bhaktiyoga* is arbitrary. She thinks for it only after getting fulfilled with her household responsibilities. On the other hand, Urvashi Devi's *Bhaktiyoga* is not as random in comparison to Anuradha's spirituality. Her actions are unmotivated and like Mirabai she is also well-determined to proceed in the similar direction. Hence, Urvashi Devi's followers find Mirabai's reflection in her personality.

Bharati Sarabhai unearths two different contours of human mind. Two women in the play do not differ here biologically from each other. The first leads perfectly an unattached and unselfish life. But it is really exceptional. The other leads a general way of life. She is serious about salvation only after fulfilling her responsibilities. A true salvation demands a detached self from the very stage of maturity. Like Anuradha, it is not practically possible for millions of women. A true divine *bhaktiyog* is beyond their reach. Even after the decision to leave for Himalaya; Anuradha never discards the growing illness of her husband. She feels strongly that she should accompany him in his bad health.

This part of the play occupies her personal conflict and also her attempt to reach a rational conclusion. Bharati Sarabhai succeeds in dramatizing Anuradha's conflict to take any firm decision. It does not come easily to Anuradha's way. She denied earlier accompanying Kanak Raya for his Ceylon trip. The conflict in Anuradha's mind arises out of her fear for husband's poor health and craves for Himalaya. Kanak deeply feels that there are a number of issues in their relationship which were not discussed at all. He regrets for not having a transparent, delicate and affectionate relation between them. Kanak, being the king of a state and under the impression of Western traits, always repressed his wife's genuine feelings. He neglected her faith in Lord Krishna and also her desire that he should be with her in the search of God. Like Mirabai's husband Rana, Kanak Raya preferred to discourage her wife to lead the path of spirituality.

As the French Psychoanalytic Feminism attributes, the state of a woman's suppression passes through discouragement to her actions. It can be explored here through Kanak Raya's dominating behaviour. But after Anuradha's determination and his dependent state, he becomes sentimental about their relation and feels concerned for it. He speaks out:

> Once I dreamt that it was done! You wrote me a long, long letter. All our life was there...to make up for the years and years we lost each other...even the years to come. All that you had to said, not done was all there: clearly beautifully put down, without interruption, for all time—as I would have loved it to have happened. (89)

It is stepping backward after realizing the need of a true companion in life. His realization comes out only after Anuradha's determination to leave the palace in search of God. The play shows its attribution to the female phase of writing, disentangled by the foremost writer and critic Elaine Showalter as it insists for a woman's text and a woman. The disputes between husband and wife disclose the social reality in India. They spend a long married life together but with trivial contraversies. Anuradha and Kanak Raya have been living together for some years now but with misunderstanding and distrust.

Anuradha finds it difficult to leave her husband alone in his illness. It is not easy for her being a Hindu wife, to separate from Kanak and lead an isolated and uncertain path. The playwright insists here the realization of a woman. She tries to learn from the trials she undergoes in her life. Kanak Raya loses his health and desires utterly that his wife should be with him. Bharati Sarabhai encapsulates perfectly the diverse shades of Kanak Raya's state of mind here. The theme of woman's jealous and immature perception has been elaborated here with Sudha's behaviour. She hates Urvashi Devi and finds nothing radiant in her personality. Her jealous arises out of Darshan's growing concern for Urvashi Devi. Sudha's negative thinking strikes more to Shastriji, Urvashi's father. She disregards Urvashi because she considers her responsible for breaking off her engagement with Darshan. She blaims: "I'm convinced it is all Urvashi's doing! She can't marry, and she won't let others marry! I shall expose her debunk the Mira Bai myth! I don't care any more to keep these white lies" (92).

Kanaka Raya suggests for Sudha's disenchantment: "My dear child, we all have our disappointments. Why not take a more reasonable view" (*ibid.*). Sudha fails to hide her dissatisfaction over her aunt Anuradha's plan to leave for Himalaya because Kanak Raya was in bad health and required his wife. Sudha, as proclaims earlier, has a heartache experience due to break up with Darshan. She also cares lot for the health of her uncle. The playwright succeeds to craft various aspects of human personality. The hurdles in life make it difficult for Kanak Raya to listen properly the inner voice. The playwright presents it in the play with the sea metaphor.

The followers of Urvashi Devi gather at seashore and stand round. She has a magnificent impression on the minds of these followers. They consider her 'Modern Mira' as they experience an outstanding enchantment in her acompanishment. Urvashi Devi rejects submissively to be considered as Mira. There is an important aspect of relationship between Urvashi Devi and Darshan. He has a deep-longing for Urvashi Devi. He believes strongly that Urvashi has forgotten to listen her 'self' in her busy schedule. There is not any consideration for such emotional bonding in her life. Darshan observes: "There are two women in each one of you. The artist and the saint, at war with each other—and playing havoc with poor man. You are two strong, that's the trouble with you. Both of you have some wrong. Your inherited notions of good and bad have misled you, cramped you" (108). She (Urvashi Devi) should think a bit like other ordinary women who have certain expectations from life. She should not consider her life as a private enterprise. She has not enough time to care for her needs as any other woman has. Kanak Raya adds further: "When I look out you, I see two heads. As an idiot who reels, sees two where there is but one. One woman looks at me with the eyes of Urvashi, the beloved; but the other looks away with the eyes of Mira, the saint. Is she one or is she two? I think I am half-blind now. I do not know what I see" (111). The playwright is keen to elaborate here the general human tendency that forces sometime to hide one's genuine feelings out of social fear. The following dialogue between Darshan and Urvashi is quite supportive in this regard.

URVASHI : Look at me. Look into my eyes. What do you see?
DARSHAN : Deepness...
URVASHI : Is it still or is it moving?
DARSHAN : Still.
URVASHI : Come nearer. What do you see now?
DARSHAN : An image.
URVASHI : One, or two?
DARSHAN : One.
URVASHI : Whose?
DARSHAN : My own.
URVASHI : (Gently) Forget Mira Bai! Forget Urvashi!
Neither is as real as your image held
hence in my eyes. (111-12)

This is what Urvashi Devi does not want to show to the outside world. She insists Darshan to consider the moment as the lasting recognition of their relationship. Even Anuradha likes to bridge the gap between them. But fails to do it. The end of the play is tragic with Kanak Raya's death and also a wise realization on Anuradha's part. Anuradha gives up the thought of Himalyan hermitage as she decides to be with her husband in his illness. Anuradha's repentance at the end is also noteworthy. She confesses: "At first I used to think I was not right, absolutely right, *my* costumes, *my* morals, *my* Himalaya, *my* God. I thought everything different was an obstruction" (116).

The play is different from Sarabhai's maiden play *The Well of the People* in terms of a woman's individual space and her world of experience. The protagonist here does not hesitate like the old woman in *The Well of the People*, to respond firmly her inner voice. The womanhood in the play does not cripple like a bonsai plant as it does in *The Well of the People* but strives hard for existence on personal terms.

The spatial dynamics helps to explore the elements of social realism like subjugation of a woman, differences between husband and wife, the desire for isolation in the play, *Two Women*. Bharati Sarabhai tackles the gender-based issues in both the plays. The playwright uses different dramatic forms for a skillful presentation. *The Well of the People* interacts the way a woman is being forced to act according to phallocentric traits. She has to strive for salvation of male members of her family amidst poverty and crippling old age. In this way, the faith and spirituality of her society becomes her personal consideration. The playwright shows how in male-dominated power structure there isn't any choice for a woman to act according to her personal will. But to the end, Gandhi's call for unto this last helps her to listen inner voice and take decision of her choice. Bharati Sarabhai, with a skillful dramatic expression, presents how men's verdict becomes a law for women. On the other hand, *Two Women* explores a different reality about Indian womanhood. It depicts complexity of a woman in a patriarchal society and also shows woman's ability in taking personal decisions. It is a perfect observation of restrained Indian womanhood in phallocentric structure of Indian society of pre-Independence phase. Mahasweta Devi whereas reveals Indian womanhood by interpreting Indian motherhood in the plays *Mother of 1084* and *Bayen*.

II

Mahasweta Devi (b. 1926), a well-known activist-writer, retains a prestigious position for the idiosyncrasy related to practical writing. She has been working to change the lot of tribal people in the states such as Bihar, West Bengal, Madhya Pradesh, Chhattisgarh and Odisha. Though, her literary activism is restricted to certain regions; she does not consider herself as a writer of a particular state. She mentions: "...all my books could represent India. I consider myself an Indian writer because what I am writing could be true of any part of India" (Dickman: 34). In this way, her literary distinctiveness is not a flash in the pan but an outcome of her comprehensive expression. The unfailing commitment for the upliftment of 'the wretched of the earth' is soul of her writing. In her oeuvre, there is a depiction of brutal oppression of tribal people and the untouchables by potent, authoritarian upper-caste landlords, lenders, and several government officials showing its relation with an age-old history of domination. Noted Neo-Marxist critic, George Luckas, finds depiction of reality as the real criterion of greatness of every great writer. Likewise, Mahasweta Devi undoubtedly shows an indominatable faith in Luckas and Brecht also when she accepts the fact that literature should function extensively for people's emancipation struggle. Her literature, in this way, is more like a river in the plain than a gushing cascade.

Born in Dhaka to literary parents in a Hindu Brahmin family, Mahasweta Devi completed her schooling in Dhaka but after the partition of India she moved to West Bengal. Mahasweta Devi's first literary contribution *The Queen of Jhansi* is a biography of the great queen warrior. Her other works are *Mother of 1084, The Occupation of the Forest, Bitter Soil, Dust on the Road, Our Non-Veg Cow, Bashai Tudu, Breast Stories, The Book of the Hunter,* etc. She was awarded with Sahitya Akademi award for the Best Writers in 1979 for her work *Aranyer Adhikar*. She was awarded with Padmashree in the year 1986. The highest literary award Jnanpith was awarded to her in the year 1996. She was awarded with Raman Magasaysay Award for Journalism, Literature, and Creative Communication in the year 1997. The second highest civilian award Padma Vibhushan was confronted on her in the year 2006. Moving to her dramatic contribution, she wrote five plays in two different phases of playwrighting in her career. Out of them, *Mother of 1084*, her maiden play and *Bayen* are chosen here to respect her concern for woman's subjectivity and gender-centred reality.

The play, *Mother of 1084,* depicts the social reality with a background of Naxalite activities in Kolkata of the late seventies. Elaborating its subject, Raghu Paraghi (2009: 43) comments: "Mahasweta Devi's *Mother of 1084* is set in the background of the Naxalite movement in West Bengal, focusing on the economical and social exploitation in rural as well as urban areas." The playwright unearths here the stages of suffering, torture of the young educated people in Kolkata. The Naxalbari movement was initiated to fight for the rights of peasants and the workers in industries. The ruling class was responsible mainly for inhumanity with these people. The young generation, under the impression of Lenin and Karl Marx's ideology came together to finish inequality based on socio-economical condition. It was a Herculean task to challenge the prevailing system for an expected change. But these young aspirants with an indomitable spirit began to work for an ideal socio-political scenario. The domination on socio-political as well as economical fronts was extremely horrible. Even after the Independence there was not any positive change in the lives of underdogs. The leaders of this movement were firm to change the system and create a new world of equality and justice.

The play, on the other hand, unearths a mother's journey from ignorance to knowledge. The journey of protagonist is a *Bildungsroman* depicting writer's enriching social concern. Sujata, Brati's mother, like millions of Indian women is completely ignorant of her son's mission for betterment of oppressed people, promising an unto this last development. The purpose of the movement was to ensure change in the lives of millions of sufferers under the inhuman political, social, and economical strategies. In this way, Sujata is not merely an individual but representative of those ignorant people who rather curse the young people for their unproductive engagements. The bureaucrats, diplomats, and other high class people were keen to suppress the genuine urge of this movement. They misinterpreted the logical concerns of the leaders and members of the movement, considering the young people as culprit or blot on the social life. It resulted in obtaining a modest support from the common men and women in our society.

The play *Mother of 1084* deals with the Naxalite movement and aftermath. Sujata Chatterjee, protagonist of the play, a *bhadralok* (bourgeoisie) family member lives in a sound socio-economical condition. But her family happiness is just a skin-deep. The play proceeds through Sujata's realization of truth after two years of her son, Brati, a Naxalite insurgent's death. Sujata comes out of her cocoon and meets first Somu's mother and then Nandini to realize that Brati was not a criminal. In this way, Sujata's journey transforms her from a hopeless dependent to a hopeful independent. Her son marched on his ideals and sacrificed his life for a sublime purpose. No one in the family, except his mother Sujata tries to understand his mission and trust his ideals. The last scene in the play, a party scene, symbolically deals with Sujata's liberation by signifying her support to Brati.

The play opens with a phone call from the police morgue. It was to identify Brati, the young member of the family. Sujata, Brati's mother receives the call and remains confused for some time. The voice on the phone asks:

VOICE : Who are you?

SUJATA : (surprised). Mrs Chatterjee

VOICE : Mrs Dibyanath Chatterjee?

SUJATA : Yes. Who are you? ...

VOICE : What's Brati Chatterjee's relationship with you?

SUJATA : Son.

VOICE : Son? Come to Kantapukur. (3)

Sujata Chatterjee is unaware of the details communicated to her on the phone. Samik Bandyopadhyay (1990: vii) comments: "A working mother, for whom her work is in itself a form of protest and self-assertion against the patriarchal authority of her husband, discovers only too late that her son is part of the Naxalite movement when she is summoned one morning to identify his dead body in the police morgue." On the other hand, the very name Kanatapukur makes everything clear before Dibyanath Chatterjee, Brati's father. He does not want to show his relation with Brati. Sujata wants to take the car out for Kantapukur but Dibyanath does not allow it. He does not show any concern for his son, Brati's death. His reaction after the news of son's death is not usual. He never laments for the demise of his son as the other fathers usually do. But unnaturally he tries to save his image from deformation. It surprises one to see the way he gets support from his elder son, Jyoti. He, like his father, has no faith in the ideology of social equality. Even Brati's sister has not any inclination to the initiatives of Brati. Both of them are not interested at all to know his mission or co-operate him anyway possible. They are not comfortable with Brati's ideals, actually. They believe that his mission for social equality is just a day-dreaming. Brati is not going to prove anything for anybody. But Sujata considers her son equally important and liable. She finds extra-ordinary qualities in Brati because he lives for the sake of others.

Sujata identifies Brati's dead body but the police officer on duty does not allow her to take it to have for cremation. In this way, she is not allowed to perform the last rituals of her dear son. The Kolkata police in late seventies went on suppressing any kind of action of these educated young people. The members of the movement were inspired by Karl Marx and Lenin's ideals. The educated middle-class young people like Brati dreamt an ideal, independent society. They considered it as their responsibility to create a modern society completely based on social equality. It was a sign of danger for the bureaucracy, politics of that time to see the movement getting a wider support from the different walks of life. The police with an intention to spread terror among the young people and their families to withdraw any kind of support to this movement, continued to strangle the spirit of the movement. The dead bodies of the Naxalites were not allowed to take away for the last rituals. Actually, it was a well-thought plan to stop the growing enrollment of the youngsters to the movement. Sujata's journey from the state of ignorance to knowledge is an unexpected, unbelievable reality for the women of bourgeoisie community; content to stay in their ivory towers. They prefer negligence to attention. Sujata's voyage becomes a transgression of family boundaries to enter public arena.

She understands oppression, resistance, and her son's true nature for the first time. Sujata's transformation begins only after her dear son Brati's brutal encounter in the mob attack. The state of ignorance of women like Sujata, compels Nandini to comment on the passivity of a domestic woman like Sujata. Exactly after two years of Brati's death, i.e. on 17 January Sujata receives a call from Nandini. It means Sujata's voyage to unearth the cause behind Brati's death begins exactly on the same date of his birth. She meets Somu's mother on the same day and tries to know more about her son. In her meeting with Somu's mother and Nandini, Sujata realizes that she knows little about her son in comparison to Nandini and Somu's mother. She might have forgotten that "Motherhood demands not only love and care, but also understanding and possibility of communication between mother and child" (Chakravarthy: 107). It takes a long time for Sujata to percept her son's mission and to extend her support to him. Brati sacrifices his life for the happiness of less-privileged people in society. But on the other hand, it is not so that she is completely ignorant of Brati's humane nature and his beliefs. Except Sujata, no one in the family understands Brati's genuine sentiments. They often make a fun of his ideals and consider the young generation of Brati's type is rather violent and outspoken with the material prosperity of the modern time. But Sujata considers Brati is more sublime than others. The traditional view of self-surrender can be challenged by the psychological interpretations. It analyzes a mother's character by showing an indomitable confidence in her personality. Sujata neither surrenders nor accepts Brati being blamed by other family members. But at the same time, she attempts to explore the real, unfelt aspect of his personality. It is mother in Sujata that gives enough support to stand against the views of her family members. On the other hand, Brati expects nothing from his siblings as he might have believed that 'blessed is he who expects nothing for he shall never be disappointed'. The prejudiced opinion of her family members forces Sujata to mention: "Brati was dead to all of you long before, isn't that so?" (9).

Sujata's visit to Somu's house is a devastating experience as one awakens after a frightful dream. Somu belongs to a lower middle-class family. But, beyond social class, stature and gender there exists an emotional bond between Sujata and Somu's mother. They are mothers of sons who have lost their lives in a mob encounter. Therefore, their sorrow has a similar language of expression. They connot their utmost grief for the loss of their sons. But it is their social class that decides their future move. Somu's mother like Sujata does not undertake any mission to find the reasons behind her son Somu's death due to unavoidable toil for the daily requirements of family members. Sujata, being in a sound economical condition, finds enough time to commence a journey to know the cause behind Brati's death. Mahasweta Devi, in this way, illustrates the socio-economical inequality to ascertain the meaning of motherhood. It was quite difficult for Somu's parents to consider except their family requirements. But Somu's mother has similar sorrow like Sujata's after her son's death. She replies: "Quite, sister? How can there be quiet with the mother's hearts burning like bodies on fire?" (10). Mothers like Sujata are mostly unaware of the outside activities of their sons and daughters. Their ignorance is mostly responsible for this unexpected or unbelieveble experience.

Sujata understands her son, Brati's mission for the first time. Her long discussion with Somu's mother gives her complete information of Brati's mission. Being a mother, it was her responsibility to keep the details of Brati's doings. She never knew that Somu's home was the headquarter of Brati and his comrades' outside operations. Brati's simple, humanistic nature appeals a lot to Somu's mother. She reminds: "...He'd come and call out Mashima, a cup of tea please, a glass of water! Sweet words" (11). Brati's affectionate nature created a place for him in the hearts of others. He gave up his life for his comrades by visiting Somu's house that night with a purpose. The mob attacks and kills them brutally. Among his movement friends, Brati's simplicity and loving nature were the most appealing qualities of his personality. It was Anindya's responsibility to inform Somu and others and later on report the same to Brati. Anindya cheated them by informing their whereabouts to the police. It was a betrayal on the whole. Brati and his comrades dared to face the mob because they might have believed in the dictum 'better to die on your feet than live on your knees'. The police appear on the scene after the incident.

Sujata's visit to Nandini is the crucial scene in the play. Sujata comes to know a lot of things about Brati only after this meeting. Nandini tells Sujata about the police torture and also the way they were betrayed. Nandini helps, Sujata, in this way, to experience the reality.

Sujata appeals the audience to awake and undestand the reality at the party scene. Sujata discovers the real world of her son which is completely different than anybody around her. She addresses:

Where is the place where there's no killer, no bullets, no prison, no vans? (*Goes round the stage.*) Where can you escape it all, Brati, in Calcutta, in West Bengal, from north to south, from east to west? You can't be on the run any longer, Brati. Brati, come back. ...let it tear down the happiness of everyone cooped up in his own happy happiness. (31)

Brati's intentions were certainly clear. Brati's life ideals were modeled on Marx and Lenin's philosophy of social equality.This ideology was base of their actual social operation. Well-being of suppressed, pathetic people was his life motto. Sujata, in her journey, not only explores the world of her son but also gets an objective for remaining life. Her journey becomes a perpetual experience leading her from unknown to known. Sujata's journey for truth ends with her self-discovery. In this way, Mahasweta Devi looks at the Naxalite movement from an upper middle and lower class perspective. The women like Sujata do not know more about the social and political changes taking place outside. The Naxalite initiative to change the social, political, and economical situation and also the forceful attempt of bureaucracy and rich professionals to suppress the movement was completely unknown to these women. It is Mahasweta Devi's introspection, presented in the form of Sujata's journey regarding ignorance of bourgeoisie women for the external world. By and large, *Mother of 1084* is written with a strong socio-political background of Naxalite movement. It depicts a woman's attempt to discover the outside realities and identifies the self during the course of her journey. On the other hand, the playwright offers a strong criticism on complete negligence of bourgeoisie women for the outside realities.

Mahasweta Devi goes a few steps ahead to discover the gender centric social realism with an utter humanistic observation in *Bayen* (1976), the other play for the study. Talking about subject of the play, Samik Bandyopadhyay (*ibid*.: xii) comments: "...*Bayen*, in which a mother is branded as a witch and separated from her son till the latter acknowledges the dead woman as his mother, lies deeper than the obvious protest the inhumanity of superstition." The play consists just four scenes. Within its concise structure; it knits different dimensions that unearth the stages of social oppression. The playwright shares her genuine concern for the character of Chandidasi. The playwright is with her protagonist less for being a woman but more for being a human. Mahasweta Devi, in her short stories and novels does not sympathize with her woman protagonists out of a gender concern only. But it is more a humanistic favour. Chandi, the protagonist of the play, journeys from vocation to apotheosis through trauma and elaborates thus, a woman's constant, unavoidable fight in a male-dominated society. These stages, central to scene I, II, III and IV in the play, take her life from an unavoidable strife to a deserved subjectivity. Mahasweta Devi through Chandidasi's tragic tale raises the issue of woman's suppression, considering it as an aspect of gender-based social reality.

The age-old concepts of superiority and inferiority have been dominating our society to a great extent. A woman with an utmost dedication discharges her ancestral duties in a male-dominated society. She considers the job of 'grave-keeping' as God's work and it becomes her vocation. She takes sincere efforts to perform her duties. But instead of realizing her dedication and sacrifice, the society continues to insult her by defaming her as a witch. No one acknowledges her greatness or outstanding efforts in performing ancestral duty. She has been compelled to live pariah on the basis of Necromancy, the magic of communicating with the souls of the dead to obtain useful information. This ancient form of magic is really unknown to Chandi's simple, innocent personality. She has been performing her duties honestly but no one cares to heed her sentiments.

The various kinds of superstitions have been responsible for ruining the life of thousands of innocent people. In most of the cases, women are the victims of this cruelty. The social evils in India are entrenched so deeply that cutting one root would not be sufficient to stop its effects. Mahasweta Devi has reported that any strange thing or event can be attributed to the witches and they can be killed with popular approval. Majority of the victims are women and it is estimated that 600 women are killed annually on this charge. Debashish Chattopadhyay (2008: 105) has appropriate words to ascertain Mahasweta Devi's concern to unearth plight of women in Indian society. He mentions:

> ...Mahasweta Devi, the most distinguished social activist among the contemporary Bengali literary artists, took up her pen to explore and explode the sham and fraudulence of the democratic set-up in our community and to represent the fates of marginalized women undergoing untold miseries within and without their own communities.

The play *Bayen* (1976) is based on a woman's constant suffering in the male-dominated world. Chandidasi, the protagonist, belongs to Gangaputta's and Gangadasi's clan. She continues the ancestral job of burying dead children after her father's death. She marries Malinder, a Dome and gives birth to Bhagirath. She confronts an ideological conflict between a mother's responsibility and ancestral accountability after giving birth to a child. She loses her mental balance and the community ostracizes her on the charge of a bayen thereafter. To the end, she immolates her life while stopping a passenger train from disaster and her son, Bhagirath declares that Chandidasi Gangadasi was not a bayen but his mother.

The play opens with Chandi's reminiscence. She sings and tells:

> My child god sleeps in my lap...in my lap... (Stops singing).
>
> I don't have anybody any more, nobody.
>
> When I hadn't become a Bayen, I had everybody. (75)

Her retrospection shows her affinity for her child and also her pathetic condition after losing the shelter of right. Now, past is nothing but a metaphor of soar experience to her. It has been affecting the whole of her life. She is forced to leave her family members for no fault on her part. Her sacrifice of motherhood is rewarded with an imposition as a pariah. With ostracization, her husband's affection also begins waning, substantially. Ignorance of the people, their superstitious traits were mainly responsible for Chandi's pathetic condition. She is labeled as a bayen, a witch and considered as the most inauspicious creature. Chandi juxtaposes two contrasting images here. She is a care-taking, nurturing woman who keeps the graves risking her life. But at the same time, she is a witch for the society. She possesses now the black magic. Though she knows it very well that she is like other common women, the fear of having an extraordinary powers causes difficulties in her personal life. Naturally, her mother's image resonates affection, kindness, and love. But the enforced image accentuates evil in her personality. She is a witch, an evil doer now. One who raises the dead children to suckle them. The cunning society snatches a mother from a woman for no personal fault. According to Radha Chakravarthy: "Chandi is a figure of sacrifice and self-denial" (*ibid.*: 99). But society generally follows a negative, harmful way to acknowledge a woman's power. Chandi is ostracized, separated from her son on the charge of black power. Instead of supporting her extraordinary strength of keeping the graves throughout the night, without any fear; she receives in return the award of ostracization. The phallocentric society finds it difficult to accept any woman's outstanding qualities. It reacts generally in a negative sense of mind. For deconstruction, identity is viewed not longer a stable, fixed, or pre-given essence but dependent on circumstances. Similarly, Chandi's recognition swiftly converts with changing outside situations. She strives to establish herself as mild, sensitive, woman but her identity relies largely on the will of leaders of community in which she lives. They do not care her urge but continually construct her adverse image. The community suppresses her abilities through mental torture and inferior language. They start to propagate now that Chandi is solely responsible for whatever worst is taking place in the lives of villagers. She is not allowed to look at any child. Even at her own son, Bhagirath due to evil sight. She has to look on the ground and hit the canister constantly while passing through the locality. Her community expected to discharge her ancestral duties, honestly but did not allow casting a sight of her son. Her affection for Bhagirath is natural but no one heeds it. In this way, Mahasweta Devi "...touches the larger space of the social forces that separate mother and son in a male-dominated system" (*Five Plays*: xiii).

Chandi, living in isolation, could not suppress her deep, unquestionable longing for Bhagirath like many other mothers in the world. But the upper-class lord Gourdas had nothing to do with her sincerity and also her desire to perform a mother's responsibilities. Referring the Freudian notion *Repression*, her natural desires are suppressed and she is forced to perform the social responsibility given to her.

Malinder becoming the member of dominaters' party, discredits Chandi's forgo of *pleasure principle* to discharge ancestral duties with a preference and honesty. Later on, Malinder frees his sentiments before Bhagirath to experience *Catharsis*/Purgation. He tells him: "She had everything when she was your mother, my wife. I gave her striped saries to wear, and silver nickelled jewellery. I fed her, I rubbed oil in her, her body (sighs)" (78). Malinder is pleased to tell his son that Chandi's forebears were rewarded with all the cremation grounds of the world by Harishchandra, the king.

Chandidasi finds it difficult to look after her child due to her job of grave digging and keeping. She feels strongly that she should give up the job to take care of her child. She tells her husband: "It hurts to do the job these days, the job handed down to me by my ancestors, my hands rebel, and yet I have to go on doing it" (82). Her preference to Bhagirath's nourishment is not responded positively because Malinder expects that Chandi should care more for her job than her responsibilities of a mother. He satisfies her with the words: ".... When a child dies, can anyone keep it in the house? The job you do is a useful one but the bastards won't recognize that" (82). In patriarchal society the sentiments of women are often neglected. They are satisfied by reminding them their duties. Repression of a woman's desire in patriarchal society converts automatically in restricting her natural right of taking decision. Chandi cannot think like Malinder because she fails to hide her affection for Bhagirath, her child. In this way, this stage of her life is with full of trauma received in patriarchy. She has to look after her child and also perform the ancestral duty, assigned to her. She has to keep the graves during nights, look after her child and satisfy her husband's desire. But, unfortunately except humiliation nothing comes to her way.

The members of the society disregard Chandi's efforts and leave her to suffer by forcing to live as a pariah. Gayatri Chakraborty Spivak, the translator of Mahasweta Devi's short-stories, finds a striking resemblance among her women protagonists. From Spivak's point of view, Mahasweta Devi deals with the poverty-stricken, suppressed women belong to lower classes from a humanistic point of view. To add further: "Mahasweta Devi is different from both Tendulkar and Dattani in that she focuses on the link between the feudalistic set up and patriarchy" (Thankamma: 47).

Chandi's lives with a dilemma whether she should continue the ancestral job or leave it and look after Bhagirath. She expresses her dilemma in following words: "...I seem to hear my father's voice roaring like thunder: If you opt out, it'll be my beat again, is that what you desire? I can almost hear him chasing the jackals away, thundering all the while, hoi! hoi! hoia!" (83).

Chandi is half-hearted to response the blames for Tukni's death. She loved Tukni as her daughter. But very easily her affection for Tukni is forgotten. Tukni is her cousin Pakhi's daughter. Actually, Tukni died of small-pox. No medical treatment was given to her. Unavailability of the treatment at a proper time caused her unfortunate death. She was given some herbals. Shashi, her brother-in-law along with Pakhi blamed her for Tukni's death. The loss of mental order forces Chandi to behave in a strange manner. The terrific humiliation causes physical as well as psychological isolation from the society she belongs.

Bhagirath feels her mother's love and care naturally. Therefore, he starts visiting her hovel but Chandi dislikes his visits. A mother's heart compels to meet Malinder to warn Bhagirath not to visit her hovel again. She is on the way to Malinder. Gourdas and his followers lay down a pile of bamboo to loot the train. Chandi gets death while averting the train but saves thousands of lives and proves, in this way that she is not a witch or bayen but similar to millions of other women with full of affinity for humankind. Bhagirath identifies the dead body as his mother, Chandi before the government officials. In this way, Bhagirath's open declaration grants an apotheosis stature to her. She risks her life to save those people who ostracize her. The community separates a mother from her child. But she does not think to revenge against the society as she acts courageously to save their life. A supernatural quality, i.e. humanity in her personality differentiates her from others. Mahasweta Devi illustrates Chandi's superhuman qualities to show how the basic values in her such as kindness, generosity do not disappear in the midst of social humiliation. Chandi sacrifices her life while averting the train from a mishap. She becomes a martyr for the society. No one acknowledges her sanguine efforts, earlier. But she obtains now an apotheosis position. The people who tormented her now find God's image in her personality after her son Bhagirath comes out and accepts Chandi as his mother.

The play arouses readers' sentiments due to the potentials to discover a woman's real world. Mahasweta Devi explores the cruelty of superstition that causes ultimately death of the sufferer but before that a worst, unbearable life. Certain superstitions still prevails in tribal communities leading ultimately to death. Mostly the women are victim of such phallocentric subsumptions. No one takes in consideration their innocence and they are strangled to death. The playwright depicts the reality in the communities of less-privileged with an utmost concern and strives in this way to empower the powerless. To put in nutshell "By lending voice to the voiceless, Mahasweta emerges as a fighter for human rights" (Dasan: 132). The play, *Bayen,* is a crest of Mahasweta Devi's literary excellence and an emblem of her altruistic engagements. Mahasweta Devi in both the plays for the present study explores such a world of women where the motherhood relies largely on patriarchal notions. But at the same time, their concern for motherhood frees them from these restrains. On the other hand, Manjula Padmanabhan takes a more realistc stand to explore woman's social stature in her plays.

III

Manjula Padmanabhan is a playwright, journalist, comic strip artist, children's book writer and author of the the play *Harvest*. She has also written plays such as *Lights Out* (1986), *Hidden Fires* (solo by Rashi Bunny), *The Artist's Model* (1995) and *Sextet* (1996). The novels and short stories of Padmanabhan explore the different aspects of contemporary realities, centring woman's stature. Her dramatic genius lies in her efforts to recreate theatre as an open-ended process than a finished product.

Born in Delhi to a diplomat family, she went to boarding school in her teenage. She has authored a collection of short stories, called *Kleptomania*. Her recently published and thoroughly discussed book is *Escape* (2008). Apart from writing newspaper columns, she created also comic strips. She created Suki, an Indian female comic character, which was serialized as a strip in *Sunday Observer*. Before 1997 (the year in which her play *Harvest* was staged) she was better known as cartoonist and had a daily cartoon strip in *The Pioneer*, a daily. The interpretation here is limited to her plays *Lights Out* and *Harvest* centring her disquiet for social reality with a forceful interrogation of woman's position in the contemporary life. The play *Lights Out* (1986) is based on an eyewitness account. It comprises the incident took place in Santa Cruz, Mumbai, in 1982. Molestation of a woman continues over a period of weeks, a group of middle-class people go on discussing the event without performing any kind of action to stop it. The group includes women also who bother the noise and not the non-humanity with a woman. On the other hand, the men speak in their gender prejudiced discourse. They prefer to make an issue of a woman's non-chestity after the rape than any kind of help. They plan to bit the molesters but do not dare to leave their premises. To the end, police rushes to the spot and the goondas runaway. In this way, the play highlights typical middle class mentality of futile discussions.

Manjula Padmanabhan strikes here the way a woman's issue is being treated in our so-called sophisticated society. No one comes out to punish the evildoers but discusses and enjoys from their gallery. The middle-class men and women just make an issue of a woman's molestation for their time pass discussions.

Men enjoy a woman is being molestated whereas women have not enough strength to take any meaningful action to stop the crime or to make a phone call to the police. Here they prefer to pass useless comments from their self-knitted, comfortable cocoon. Leela urges continuously her husband to call the police and stop the ongoing noise. But her husband Bhaskar, prefers to neglect her urge. It has been a simplest strategy practiced by men to assuage significance of a woman's yearning. Molestation of a woman is a minor, negligible offence for men like him. Bhaskar is damn sure about police delay to catch the goondas. The police and Bhaskar represent typical male-centred ethos where the issues of women are subordinated. Women lack any social significance therefore any kind of injustice with them does not carry any importance for middle-class men like Bhaskar and also law and order system. Leela bothers the constant noise being created night after night. It becomes difficult for children to get proper sleep. She is more anxious about her children's and her own sleep. She mentions: "Why do they have to do it here? Why can't they go somewhere else"? (141). Generally, a sophisticated, well-settled Indian does not show any involvement in public matters. The constant screaming, coming out from nearing compound of Leela and Bhaskar's flat troubles Leela. But the negligence of Bhaskar is the fact that men in general are habitual of discaring issues of women. There is a sense of superiority in giving a marginal deliberation to women in family matters. A Marxist-feminist trait illustrates the gender-based social reality. It talks about socially-constructed image of women. Referring this trait, it can be argued that a woman inside as well as outside the home is a socially-constructed biological figure. Leela's urge is not noticed at all but it is kept aside easily on the basis of woman's inferior social construction. Bhaskar plays very easily with Leela's belief. He comments: "Some one told Leela that to watch a crime and do nothing is to be...what? Involved in it yourself?" (149). The discussion between Bhaskar and Leela is a representative of middle-class husband-wife interaction. It shows their refusing mentality to avoid social responsibility. Unrisky detachment is preferred to risky attachment.

Bhaskar's guest Mohan from Delhi arrives to stay for a night. He too resonates similar prejudiced views after listening a woman's screaming from the outside. He does not find any difficulty in watching it as a spectaculous scene. A woman's molestation is a free of cost entertainment for him. The crime taking place in a nearing compound, the urging cry of the woman does not bother Mohan and Bhaskar alike. He joins Bhaskar's company to fool Leela for her useless sentiments. Both Bhaskar and Mohan prove the fact that men irrespective of their social class are one and the same. They think seldom in favour of a woman and violence against her as they hesitate to come out and protect her. A woman is being tormented but it does not cause any trouble to both of them. Molestation of a woman is nothing except an entertainment to them. Manjula Padmanabhan signifies typical bourgeois mentality where a woman's molestation is not considered as a serious issue in this part of the play. The power of ideology in a patriarchal society always supports the inimical construction of a woman. Therefore, there is an ancillary treatment to the issues related to woman's social subsistance. Bhaskar and his friend, Mohan do not hesitate to discuss the scene before Leela.

> BHASKAR : They start off clothed and then begin to lose them.
>
> MOHAN : All of them? The assailants too?
>
> BHASKAR : Well, the assailants tear the clothes off the victims and then, perhaps in the general excitement remove their own's clothes as well. (157-58)

Leela interrupts their futile, inhumane discussion and interrogates: "Oh, but why, why are we talking about this thing" (158). The possibility of saving the victim from brutality depends particularly on the spot police action. But Bhaskar does not show any kind of interest in calling the police, though Leela continuously insist to help the victim. Neutrality of the so-called sophisticated men like Bhaskar and Mohan troubles playwright's cultured mind. Instead of performing their duty, the so-called sophisticated individuals show their cheap mentality through meaningless discussions. Mohan's illogical and irritating conclusion that whatever is going on in the nearing compound is just a ritual. Hence, it discloses middle-class mentality of avoiding responsibilities. He mentions: "That would explain why no one goes to the help of the victims...even the police" (159).

The people like Bhaskar, Mohan and Surrinder find it possible to escape by considering the sound as a part of rituals. In this way, they link a woman's molestation with a religious ceremony. It is an easiest way to avoid responsibility. At the same time, they do not give up any chance to prove themselves 'decent'. But Naina questions: "...what is the point in being decent?" (175). The men boasting their strength should have left their premise to help the victim but any practical help of the victim does not take place. In a male-dominated society, a woman seems to be helpless. She is not allowed to interfere in public matters as well as she has been compelled to follow men instead of doing anything on her part. Individuality of a woman, thus, stands nowhere. She experiences a great difficulty in stating her views under male-dominance.

Bhaskar, Leela and their friends could easily isolate themselves from doing anything to stop the crime on this basis of considering molestation as a ritual. Bhaskar does not hesitate to mention: "They're like animals, really. Decent people like us; we can't understand their lives at all" (177).

The futile discussion among Mohan, Bhaskar and Sudhir displays their ordinary level of thinking. They decide to come down and visit the place and flash the incident. How terrific it is to see the so-called cultured people planning to make money by selling the photos of the incident to the press. Mohan does not feel any kind of shame to add; "...pictures like these, even the foreign press would snap them up...of a gang rape in action?" (178). It is disgusting to know their tactic of selling the photographs to media. It is a paradigm of the way issues of women are being responded by the so-called decent people. It is their mean, low-profiled attitude. It is even more hazardous to experience similar tendency of women also. Leela is serious about screaming not because she is anxious for a woman's molestation but more because she is unable to get proper sleep. It seems as she has nothing to do with crime and injustice with the woman. Rather she enjoys it. Therefore, she never hesitates to comment to the end of the play: "Oh! Then it must be over for the tonight" (189). Naina, on the other hand, is sympathetic but could not stop from enjoying the molestation. Manjula Padmanabhan conveys here different aspects of typical bourgeois life in a metropolitan city like, Mumbai which shatters to its reader and audience alike. It is Manjula Padmanabhan's subtle observation of middle class tendency that makes the play a realistic presentation.

The play *Lights Out* documents a real incident that took place in Santa Cruz, Mumbai. It depicts the aspects of human attitudes with a real, straightforward approach. Manjula Padmanabhan shows how a woman's molestation is being treated in our so-called sophisticated society. The playwright discloses here the multifarious aspects of violence. Actually, violence "...is a coercive mechanism to assert one's will over another, in order to prove or feel a sense of power" (Chitnis: 15). The fruitless discussions and harmful comments of bourgeois men and women in the play is also a kind of violence. It hurts particularly the moral code of conduct. Some time it is more dangerous than its physical formation. Without providing any help, people take pleasure in futile, meaningless discussions. It is proved through their behavior that the matter of a woman's molestation is not really serious for them. They hesitate even to call the police and save the women from brutality. Being a leading contemporary Indian playwright, Manjula Padmanabhan presents here a realistic, hypocritical world of bourgeois mentality before her readers. In this way, *Lights Out* becomes an illustrious play in the galaxy of Indian English Drama.

Manjula Padmanabhan's Aristotle Onasis Award winning futuristic play *Harvest* (1997), is a straightway attack on commodification of Third World bodies to serve the purpose of diplomatic, rich First World traders. It discloses the most disgusting form of occult economy, the twenty-first century global capitalism. Besides, it highlights a woman's subordinate position in the phallocentric system.

The play centres around Om, a chawl-resident and his family living in Mumbai. After being fired off from clerical job, he signs a bond of organ sell with a foreign company, Inter Planta. In this way, he promises all material pleasures to his wife Jaya, Ma and brother Jitu by paying a heavy price in form of selling his valuable organs. The company provides his family with all comforts by leaving them for a perpetual distress. Ginny, the leader of receiver's party controls the lives of Om and his family members with a constant communication through a contact modular.

To the end, Jaya determines to finish her life instead of allowing her organs for plantation. Symbolically, it is failure of a woman in a male-dominated society that puts her in a helpless situation. The play with a realistic treatment, presents the twenty-first century conception of dominance of First World on Third World through organ trafficking.

The playwright divides her characters in three categories, mainly. These categories are: Donors, Guards-Agents and Receivers. Manjula Padmanabhan shows a conflict between First and Third World countries by classifying her characters as donors and receivers. Om, a Third-World individual accepts the proposal of organ selling without any hesitation because it is the only way to solve many problems in his day-to-day life. He is in position now to get relief from his every-day struggle for money. The long-awaited comforts are offered now to his family members. Manjula Padmanabhan emphasizes the impact of TV Culture on the slum dwellers like Om and Ma who find their life incomplete without these electronic gadgets. Therefore, Om commodifies his body and accepts without any vacillation, the First-World dominance. Occult economy prepares his mind to the extent that he finds no other option than offering his organs to Inter Planta. The most striking feature of modern society as Manjula Padmanabhan observes in *Harvest* is its alienation from emotion, feelings, and moral values. There is not earlier generations' affection for each other between innate relations even. The growing greed for money and endless thirst for material pleasures have brought the contemporary life to a disastrous juncture. To précis, it is a lost situation. The contemporary life has caught in a maze of greed and hence finds it difficult to come out. Manjula Padmanabhan visualizes in her futuristic play that organ plantation would be an institutionalized and well-known business in Mumbai of 2010. In this way, the twenty-first century offers a new profession of organ plantation, promising all the material possessions to Third-World people, living amidst extreme difficulties.

The futuristic profession of organ plantation is a new form of global capitalism. Om and his family members have an invincible desire for money and material gains. They aspire to grab those pleasures without hard work or efforts. They move to seize the long-awaited, pleasures by selling organs. Manjula Padmanabhan sees it as a result of millennial capitalism that allows a Third-World individual to see his/her body as a selling part.

Karl Marx in his historical text *Das Capital* elaborates that the European capitalism emerged after Industrial Revolution. He discovers the ways of First-World economical dominance over Third-World countries. But in the present century, the dominance is severe to the extent that organs are offered for sale to a foreign company. "The sale of organs by the poor to the rich is a pathetic, gruesome, incident and it becomes a slay metaphor for other kinds of transaction between husband and wife, son and mother, the individual and society" (Purohit: 45). Shital Pravinchandran illustrates in her scholarly critique: "...the body, like land, is mined for its organs, and as the title of the play, I discuss below suggests, organs are removed, harvested from the body" (4). Ma does not give up any chance to prove Jaya's inferiority on the basis of her barren state. It is one of the most usual practices in Indian society to blame a woman for infertility even though she is not faulty. Dina Mehta, a prominent contemporary Indian woman playwright depicts similar reality in her celebrated social play *Brides are not for Burning*. Like Jaya, Laxmi, a newly-married woman in the play is blamed for infertility though her husband is responsible for it. The play *Harvest* entangles different relation types such as mother-in-law and daughter-in-law, mother and son, sister-in-law and brother-in-law, husband and wife and brother and brother. The play takes place in a single room. It has a firm base of complex relationship in postmodern world and also techno-generated values. For Jaya, womanhood matters more than motherhood. She determines, to the end to get her space and live her life on personal terms. Her sanctified desires of a housewife have almost suppressed. Om and Ma insult her often for trivial matters. Jaya's subjectivity is often humiliated. No one cares for her individuality. In this way, a woman confronts mostly loneliness in the family. Om's complete negligence compels her to develop an extra-marital relationship with Jitu, her brother-in-law.

The technological device such as TV compels Ma to forget her real life. After installing a TV set in her small house, she has nothing to do except watching it for hours together. Manjula Padmanabhan strikes at growing desperation of men and women for television. In this way, illusion has been preferred for reality. She is not aware of the fact that her son, Om has paid a heavy price to gain these comforts. She takes the remote in her control and becomes an addictor to unending daily soaps and films. In this way, Padmanabhan argues here the technological slavery in the postmodern world which is an important aspect of social reality.

Ginny, a smart, young agent of Inter Planta, provides all the comforts and healthy food to Om because she expects a good deal out of sell of his organs. She states:

> The most important thing is to keep Auwm smiling. Coz if Auwm's smiling, it means his body is smiling and if his body's smiling, it means his organs are smiling. And that's the kind of organs that'll survive a transplant best, smiling organs: I mean, God forbid that it should ever come to that, right? But after all, we can't let ourselves forget what this programme is about! I mean, if I'm going to need a transplant—then by God, let's make it the best damn transplant that we can manage! (229).

There is lack of affection and concern for each other in Ma and Jaya's relationship. There is no affection for each other. The relation is based on hatred and humiliation. The dialogue between them proves the lack of sympathy and affection:

> MA - Don't call me—it's your wife's turn to do the food.
>
> JAYA - It's your turn remember? I did it the last time because your programme was on (228).

In this way, Manjula Padmanabhan tackles the postmodern reality, where there is no space for inward feelings. The life is almost mechanized as the utmost feelings have dried up. Living under the same roof, people are unable to come close or develop a love relationship. The life is with full of abomination and distrust.

On the other hand, Manjula Padmanabhan deals with First-World initiatives to dominate Third-World countries. Organ plantation is part of this policy. It is interesting to see the way Ginny restrains the life of Om and his family members.

Ginny has nothing to do with Om's personal difficulties. She is anxious about his health only for the handsome amount she may get after selling his organs. She is truly a professional, well aware of market values. She also adds:

> GINNI : If Auwm's smiling it means his body's smiling. And if his body's smiling it means his organs are smiling. And that's the kind of organs that'll survive a transplant best, smiling organs.... (229).

Ginny considers donars body equal to a cash-crop. As proper care of a crop ensures greater production, similarly, appropriate concern/care of body guarantees more benefit. Om's body is important because it has a sale value now. Manjula Padmanabhan illustrates the market-oriented postmodern culture where human bodies are commodified and put them on sale.

Ma does not hesitate at all to regard Ginny better than Jaya. It is a typical Third-World mentality that finds superiority in First-World dominator and also finds nothing serious in domination purpose. Ma mentions, "You (Jaya) are just jealous of her. You don't see what a good, kind, generous, loving person—She really is" (234).

But, on the other hand, Jaya is aware of the fact that the facilities provided to them by Ginni are meant for a short period of time. Ginni is not generous but a typical professional. Therefore, Jaya insists Ma not to be habitual of watching TV, or using other electronic gadgets. She knows that the formality behind soft, delicate language of guards. They speak like trained parrots and work like honest machines. Their sophisticated language is a part of their profession.

The most striking part of the play is the way Padmanabhan introduces mother-son relationship through Ma and Jitu. It is not at all a conventional love relationship between a mother and a son. Ma has not any sympathy for Jitu or Jitu does not look for any motherly affection. When Jitu was taken for organ transplantation, her reaction remains normal.

JAYA : Ma—do you realize they've taken Jitu?

MA : ...why should I care what happens to Jeetu?

I'm through caring about anybody (242).

Ma does not consider the issue of Jitu's organ transplantation as important as her TV programme. In this way, stress in their relationship emphasizes expanding family distance and growing madness for television programmes in contemporary society.

The concluding part of the play is live and intense. Jitu is forcefully taken for organ transplantation. Now he appears before Jaya as virgil. Jaya fails to identify him. She exclaims: "you can't be. It's all just another madness" (245). But Jitu, transplanted as Virgil, explains: "This body aches for you and to give you what you yearn for" (247). But, now Jaya is not interested at all to show any kind of relation with any body. She decides now to spend her remaining life on her terms. She declares: "...enjoy myself, all by myself" (248-49).

Manjula Padmanabhan with an utmost concern for postmodern realities presents a world before her readers that differs widely from previous century morals. It is a world where there is a little scope for survival of innate relationships. There is not any ease in it as these relations are on the verge of perpetual break-up. The world is engrossed now with a thirst for material appliances that provide a momentary pleasure. The adverse effect of television on the minds of people, in other words, is an unstoppable madness. The people are distancing from each other, not to come close again. On the other hand, the playwright emphasizes here winning by losing formula that encapsulates the way Third-World poors have been losing their precious bodies to win cash. It is their predicament that they can't gain money without losing their precious bodies. To put in nutshell, Manjula Padmanabhan's *Harvest* is a realistic presentation of first-third world conflict as well as a subtle observation of changing definition of human relationships in contemporary society.On the contrary, the play explores a woman's pathetic state in family matters.

IV

The plays of Bharati Sarabhai, Mahasweta Devi and Manjula Padmanabhan elucidate woman's social stature in a male-dominated social system. The issues of women certainly receive a central concern in their plays. These playwrights emphasize women's difficulty in finding any solution to their factual condition. One comes across here the different types of experiences of women that form their gender-centred world. In this way, these plays illustrate marginalization of their voices by the dominant dramatic culture in India towards the issues of woman's existence. Bharati Sarabhai challenges the conventional, stereotyped image of Indian woman and introduces her with the new world and ideas in her plays. On the other hand, Mahasweta Devi delineates woman's identity as a mother in her plays. In this way, she depicts the way a woman takes her stand against the society when her motherhood is challenged. Manjula Padmanabhan whereas presents the urban life where a woman fails considserably to find her position in it. Thus, the creative tapestry woven by these women playwrights demonstrates the trials, rejections and endurances as well as the experimental world which Indian women share, collectively. Thus, they make an exultant, explorative revelations about their existential conditions and hold out before us is a model and unheralded chronicle of women's lives long missing in the canon of Indian English Drama. Altogether, these plays are pivotal to explore woman's stature in Indian society.

References

Bandyopadhyay, Samik (1997). *Five Plays*. Intro. Calcutta: Seagull Books.

Barret, Michele (1980). *Women's Oppression Today: The Marxist/ Feminist Encounter*. London: Verso.

Chattopadhyay, Debashish (2008). "Frames of Marginalization in Mahasweta Devi's *Outcast*: Four Stories". In Shands: 105-11.

Chakravarthy, Radha (2008). *Contemporarary Women Writers: Rethinking Subjectivity.* New York: Routledge.

Chitnis, Suma (1998). "The Concept of Violence". In Kudchedkar and Sabina: 11-18.

Dasan, M. (2004). "Writer as Fighter: Concern for Human Rights Violations in Mahasweta Devi's Plays." In Reddy and Dhawan: 75-82.

Devi, Mahasweta (1990). Bashai *Tudu*. Samık Bandyopadhyay. Intro. Kolkata: Thema.

__ (1999). *Five Plays*. Kolkata: Seagull Books.

Dhawan, R.K. and Reddy, Venkata, K. (2004). Editors. *Flowering of Indian Drama: Growth and Development of Indian Writing in English*. New Delhi: Chaman Offset Press.

Dickman, Sue (1995). "In Coversation with Indian Women Writers". *The Book Review*. 19:4 (April): 31-35.

Dr. Radhakrishnan, S. (2008). *On Mahatma Gandhi: Essays & Reflections*. New Delhi: Jaico.

Gandhi, M.K. (2000). *Woman and Social Injustice*. Ahmedabad: Navjivan Publishing House.

Keysser, Helen (1997). *Feminist Theatre and Theory*. New York: The New Case Book, Macmillan.

Kuchedkar, Shirin and Sabina, Al-Issa (Eds.) (1998). *Violence Against Women, Women Against Violence*. New Delhi: Pencraft International.

Levi-Strauss, Claude (1967). *A Structural Study of Myth and Totemism*. London.

Nandakumar, Prema (1968). "Bharati Sarabhai's English Plays." In Naik, M.K. *et al.* 191-211.

Naik, M.K. *et al.* (Eds.) (1968). *Critical Essays on Indian Writing in English*. Madras: Macmillan.

Pathan, B.A. (1984). *Gandhian Myth in English Literature in India*. New Delhi: Deep & Deep Publication.

Parghi, Raghu (2009). "Voicing Self-determination and Creating Self-Identity in Mahasweta Devi's *Mother of 1084* and Lorraine Hans Berry's *Les Blancs*." *Impression*. 2:3 (July): 44-52.

Padmanabhan, Manjula (2001). *Harvest*. Kali for Women: New Delhi.

______ (1997). *Lights Out*. Kolkata: Seagull Books.

Pravinchandran, Shital. "The Third-World Body Commodified: Manjula Padmanabhan's *Harvest.*" e-sharp Issue 8(4): 1-17.

Purohit, K. (2001). "Manjula Padmanabhan's *Harvest*: Face to Face". *The Quest,* 15(2) (Dec.): 43-46.

Sarabhai, Bharati (1942). *The Well of the People.* Calcutta: Vishva Bharati.

______ (1952). Two *Women.* Bombay: Hind Kitab Pvt. Ltd.

Sehagal, N. (1984). Cited in B.A. Pathan. *Gandhain Myth in English Literature in India.* New Delhi: Deep and Deep Publication.

Simion, Shepherd and Wallis, Mick (2004). *Drama/Theatre/ Performance.* New York: Routledge.

Shands, Kerstin W. (Ed.) (1980). *Neither East Nor West: Postcolonial Essays on Literature, Culture and Religion.* Huddinge: Sodertons.

Thankamma, Catherine (2002). "The Women Patriarchy Created: A Study of the Plays of Vijay Tendulkar, Mahesh Dattani and Mahasweta Devi." *Theatre India,* 40(2) (Nov.): 42-48.

3

The Psychodynamics of Language

> If meaning is reflected in language and mediated by experience, our knowledge of the world is potentially true knowledge.
>
> —Chris Weedon

Proceeding from the earlier to the present chapter is not just a chronological requirement. But an attempt to elaborate the matured growth of women characters from signifying patriarchal versions of world to meaningful signs. It is also an enterprise to highlight the way women protagonists have realized their socio-cultural position through an innate urge for individuality. Noted psychoanalyist Jacques Lacan emphasizes the need of social structuring of unconscious through language. He advocates the need of a different language to explore a true self. Referring his term *phallus*—a symbol of patriarchal power, Lacan insists the need to challenge it to reconstruct a different system of signification where women are equally counted. In this way, Lacan discovers a new theory consisting of revolutionary potentials. It is Lacan's comprehensive psychoanalytical impression that makes him favourite among feminist critics. Lacan mentions that the process of self-realization ends with an exploration of subjectivity. In this way, subjectivity helps to fix the meaning. He also mentions that the world of women's desire cannot be explored fully with the language of men. In this way, the concern for language of self is communicated through a liberated expression of the protagonists of the plays studied here. Their confident expression becomes the medium to release the conventional burden they have been confronting for the time immemorial. The present chapter illustrates the psychological transformations of these women protagonists to obtain the language of self-expression by realizing the fact that language is important in creativity and also leading a step ahead to accentuate Showalter's model to justify woman's world of experience, i.e. Gynocritics. Psychodynamics of woman's language, thus, shows a more radical way of subversion. On the other hand, language is an appropriate medium to illustrate gender difference. It emphasizes that how it is possible to dissociate from patriarchal dominance of writing by deconstructing male-centred discourse and reconstructing the language, centring woman's self and experience.

This magnificent journey from being signified to a meaningful sign is emphasized here through a momentous expressive transformation of these protagonists. The study accentuates also the sustaining efforts of these protagonists to have a language of one's own. But at the same time, it points out the difficulty of some women characters in freeing themselves completely from patriarchal restrictions. Julia Kristeva's Lacanian interpretations and her pioneering concept Semiotic count a special significance for a logical argumentation here. Kristeva argues that there are two important aspects of a language. One is Symbolic and the other is Semiotic. Symbolic is associated with authority, order, fathers, repression and control. On the contrary, Semiotic is characterized not by logic and order, but by displacement, slippage, condensation—suggesting looser, more randomized way of making connections, increasing the available range of possibilities. In this way, Symbolic and Semiotic are not kinds but aspects of a language. For Symbolic and Semiotic—Kristeva is indebted to Lacan's two realms—imaginary and the symbolic. Semiotic being subversive politically threatens the closed symbolic order embodied in such conventions such as governments, received cultural values, and the grammar of standard language.

The Symbolic aspect takes in consideration the patriarchal aspect of the language. The often neglected Semiotic aspect whereas covers maternity. Julia Kristeva emphasizes also that there should be a dialogical relationship between these two aspects of the language. She observes Semiotic as 'an unrepressed and unrepressive liberating energy'. It is an unending source ensuring emancipation. She asserts that women writers should adhere to it to acquire an enriching experience. On the other hand, Julia Kristeva states the details of a separatist woman's culture. She elaborates particularly Conformist and Separatist as the two major forms of feminism. According to her, the term Conformist denotes the state of women integrated into the status quo. Separatist rejects whereas a separatist woman's culture. Both the forms are considered as paranoid counter investments produced by women's exclusion from the socio-symbolic contract. The separatist culture determines the position of their 'Self' and illustrates the need of cultivating the personal stand with the help of this culture.

Feminist critics focus on Semiotic process because this process helps feminist writers to resist against phallocentrism. It helps to cultivate their own language. A direct and strong reaction against male-centred symbols and signs is possible through this 'language of self'. At the same time, reconstruction of female subjectivity can be possible with its help. It becomes indispensable to deconstruct the language as Dale Spender (2011: 121) argues in her book *Man Made Language*: "Language is not a neutral medium but one which contains many features which reflect its role as the instrument through which patriarchy finds expression." Reconstruction of the language thus becomes pivotal to constitute woman's authentic experience.

The feminist critics have found certain difficulties in creating an authentic female text. These difficulties occur due to biological, psychological, cultural and linguistic repressions. Noted feminist critic, Elaine Showalter has elaborated these forms of repression in her ground-breaking essay "Feminist Criticism in Wilderness". Sustaining the similar ideology, Julia Kristeva advocates strongly producing the resistance by returning to *Jouissance*. It is, in other words, recreation of earlier lost joy. In this way, she emphasizes the re-experience of pre-oedipal stage that guarantees a complete pleasure for women. To refer her coinage, it is an attempt to experience the physical pleasures of infancy stage, again. The psychoanalytic feminist critics insist woman writers to free themselves from the phase of oppression by observing the psychological liberation. The world of woman is beyond the possibility of exploration until one reaches to the depth of experience. The psychodynamics of women writers determines mostly the mode of their literary expression. The dissimilarity between men and women writers hence can be illustrated through the use of language. It plays a crucial role in differentiating women from men. Therefore, the specific difference between them occurs in the form of language. That's why feminist critics like Irigaray, Cixous, and Kristeva consider the language as the most specific medium to elaborate this difference. It is the language that can give women the experience of subjectivity. Women lack to represent themselves because they live in a male-centred world. The Lacanian concept 'Lack' appropriately explores the gender difference. To précis, the psychodynamics of female creativity has a preponderate relation of gender with literary creation. It initiates the process of female self-converting it into an unified, strong and liberating expression. The liberation sought is mostly a psychological transformation. The phallocentric power structure imposes an inferiority consideration over the creative minds of women. One of the models, directed to constitute an authentic female experience; the model of 'woman's psyche' propagated by Elaine Showalter helps to entangle the psychological difference at gender level. In this way, the psychodynamics of female bonding illustrates an immortal relationship among the women writers. In this way, the unified psychological state brings them together. Apprehending the psycho-feminist criticism further, it is stated that the oedipal stage damages woman's identity as it takes away the genuine female self from woman. It brings her close to the state of confusion as far determination of personal identity is concerned. The process of psychosexual differentiation lies in a child's attempt to perceive the self as separate and develop ego and body boundaries. The phallocentric ethos has insisted on the minds of readers that the Other is significant only in relation to particular. There is not any recognition for Other if the centre is excluded. Religion, philosophy, language play vital role in holding the power centre, in this way. Actually, these three spheres dominate the power structure. The psycho-feminist critics illustrate, all the way, the need of maintaining a respective position in power structure by realizing importance of self. Apart from this, they believe that language plays a vital role in power structure. At the same time, it is accepted that the symbolic discourse in various contexts is poignant to identify the actual power of men.

Language of one's own is essential because relation of an individual with society is interlinked with language. It is through language only an individual becomes the part of society. It occurs almost all the time in society that man's discourse becomes the matter of public affair. On the other hand, woman's language remains domestic hence 'trivial'. It is not an expression of decision-making. To conclude, women writers should emphasize significance of their language to make it an appropriate mode of their articulation. On the other hand, the critical interpretation of the plays here relies largely on the overstated theoretical aspect.

I

Bharati Sarabhai's maiden play, *The Well of the People* depicts an old woman's conflict to single out between imposed expression and self-expression. The difficulty to choose one out of them arises particularly due to lack of personal ability in decision-making. Conventionally, she is not expected to hold any personal discourse. Conventional mentality does not allow her easily to shift from the earlier state of mind to later. She ought to accept the male-centred discourse as her personal expression. But in the midst of it, Gandhian socio-spiritualism for the first time assists her for self-realization. It gives her enough confidence to act according to her will. She comes out with a revolutionary decision and shows her confident march towards individuality. The Gandhian ideology plays the role of a catalytic agent by helping transformation of old woman's faith. It helps her indeed to come out and accept the challenge. The decision of building a village well, communicated through chorus connotes her prepared mind, ensuring a language of self. The rational faith, she meets to the end, causes a great difficulty to single out between conventional and unconventional modes of expression. Old woman allows freely her mind for transformation of faith. Lastly, she determines to build a village well for the untouchables. She dares to speak in her own language only after realizing the self as she could not voice her repressed self for a long time. It takes a great deal of time to release her speech and communicate realization as well as subjectivity. It is shown at last with the help of a transformed self:

> Why do you go to Haridwar, to Kashi Varanasi, O my soul.
>
> What is that you seek outside? (22)

The transformed self of old woman is discovered through her changed language, denoting the spirit of liberation. The strategic difference does not occur easily. It takes considerably a long time to shift her faith. Her determination to build a well for untouchables is depicted in her confident expression:

> I shall give back, I ask you give me now Seventy rupees,—I shall work till I die. (39)

Bharati Sarabhai illustrates, in this way, a woman's difficulty in releasing herself from conventional faith in male-dominated society. Old woman's determination to accompany the path of revolution is clearly seen in her response to the chorus of peasants and workers. She does not deter to convey them the desire to build a well for the untouchables. It shatters them too much because breaking the conventional code was equal to a sin for them. They could not expect a woman preparing herself all the way to cut down the roots of custom to accept the new ideology. Old woman's decision thus offers a different world of faith. It is more rational and practical. On the other hand, Sarabhai presents contrasting attitudes of two women who are close friends of each other in the play *Two Women*. Anuradha, a queen, has a signified identity. She is known as Kanak Raya's wife instead of an individual. Urvashi, her mate whereas has a liberated self. She does not hesitate like Anuradha to determine the direction of her life. Anuradha frees herself after Urvashi's long-awaited arrival to her palace. Her arrival gives Anuradha enough strength to convey her husband the innermost passion to stay in the ageies of Himalaya. As Gandhian socio-spiritualism helps the old woman to make an insurgent decision in *The Well of the People* similarly, Urvashi Devi helps Anuradha in finding her direction. Her repressed desire, being a part of her unconscious state, comes out now with an enough strength to interact a transformed attitude. Anuradha fulfills her emotional need in the company of her best friend Urvashi. It can be argued that a woman really frees herself in the company of other woman. She shares her personal sorrow, and all those repressions in her mind which failed to find any way out in the past years. She conveys: "I have found that we live in two worlds, both shadowy, if we lack the daring to explore either of them deeply, the utmost..." (107). In this way, a woman can be a best friend of other woman. Her husband, Kanak could not recognize the difficulties of her wife. Anuradha finds it difficult earlier to interact her longing for Himalaya to her husband. Her desire becomes a part of her unconscious mind. But it receives a conscious expression only after her friend, Urvashi's long-waited arrival.

The context in which the relationship between Kanak and Anuradha forms its base requires an interrogation certainly. The lack of freedom for being Kanak's wife is responsible for disappearance of Anuradha's language. For a long time in her life, she communicates in an accepted speech. She is forced to interact in an imposed language that could not explore her self and construct individuality. Kanak Raya's interests, hobbies become her own. She fails to communicate as a woman or as an individual. In this way, she represents millions of Indian women living in male-dominated society who struggle to establish their subjectivity. Anuradha's deep concern for her lost womanhood comes out with the following expression. She conveys Kanak, her husband, her lost self and subjectivity through it. She states:

> I am field that every one has fed from and that no one has bothered about, to see that it is rested, renewed, kept green for their future crops. I have become dry. I am now barren. I resolved before my God that our daughter shall not end like this. Some times I think my life is finished. Then I see myself again, as I was, in my daughter. (22-23)

The process of female pyscho-sexual development needs to be undertaken in accordance with pre-Oedipal stage. The feminist critics Julia Kristeva, Nancy Chodorow, Lucy Irigary, and Helen Cixous have been firm to explore the authentic female experience with the help of this stage because it is not under any patriarchal impression. Nancy Chodorow argues in her seminal text *The Reproduction of Mothering: Psychoanalysis and Sociology of Gender* that the concept of mothering comprises double identification in the form of mother and child. Actually, it is a re-occurring of same mother child bond in earlier life. Anuradha has similar consideration regarding her relationship with Lata, her daughter. The childhood of her daughter becomes the mode of reappearance of Anuradha's present experience. Lata is happy in her mother's company. The mother-daughter relationship carries a great deal of importance because it denotes the psycho-sexual difference of different stages in a woman's life. Anuradha experiences a transformation after her friend Urvashi's arrival. In this way, she connects herself with pre-oedipal stage that denies patriarchal restrictions. She conveys her decision to Kanak Raya of spending the remaining part of her life in Himalaya. It is only after Urvashi's consoling, she discovers self and recognizes subjectivity. For the first time there is a change in her language because she speaks now with confidence and consideration.

It is difficult to accept an individual's experience without reproducing dominant assumptions about his/her subjectivity and language. In this way, a woman's individuality in social context can be defined. It is rather difficult to percept Anuradha's individual experience if her language and subjectivity are not reconstructed. She shows, in this way, a rare possibility to differentiate her on the basis of language and concern for subjectivity. She prefers an agreement with resistance in most of the family matters. In course of time, she looses her personal expression.

Language helps indeed to differentiate between two sexes and culture. It is necessary that language should function as a medium to express an individual's subjectivity. The language of

Anuradha is not capable enough to articulate her subjectivity. Her expression relies mostly in accordance to patriarchal discourse.

She mentions: "What her husband was to Sita. I wanted also to worship you" (19). According to Julia Kristeva, masculinity and feminity are the two aspects of a language, irrespective of biological difference. These two aspects of language rather denote tendency than biology. But Anuradha's expression preferring self does not occur easily. To the end, she decides to withdraw her plan to visit Himalaya and resolves to be with her husband in his illness. She compromises with the decision of her will for the sake of family.

Bharati Sarabhai accentuates the world of her protagonists showing their difficulty in constituting 'self' in phallocentric power structure. The process of transformation is not a cup of tea for them. But at the same time, their efforts in doing it highlight their concern for a language of self-expression. On the other hand, Mahasweta Devi distinguishes her protagonists on the basis of their self-expression after the realization of a mother's responsibilities in her plays for the study.

II

Mahasweta Devi, a leading playwright, explores the realistic state of Indian women in her plays: *Mother of 1084* and *Bayen* preferring the motherhood of her woman protagonists. Language does not stand as a barrier in Mahasweta Devi's plays. The language of her women characters is appropriate to explore their subordinate state, or to mention complete discard as subordination of women in a patriarchal society has not any specific boundaries such as region and language. Her presence in family is secondary because there is a complete negligence towards her personal expression. Her attempt is treated as 'a cry in no woman's land'.

In the conventional Indian society, domination is determined through the sex you belong. It operates beyond caste, class and race. In this way, Sujata and Chandi's subordination can be studied with similar perspecive though they belong to different social classes. Beyond their social class, their biological identity operates. For the power holders their being as a woman is the real cause of oppression. The only difference is the way their life is governed by the leaders of patriarchal system.

Sujata Chatterjee, the protagonist of *Mother of 1084* struggles initially to communicate in her own language. No one in the family seeks her advice or rights her to take personal decisions. In this way, her presence is completely neglected. To the end of the play, she comes out to speak in her own way at the party scene. Her realization helps to communicate with men and women gathered for the party. She speaks in a firm, confident discourse and succeeds in crossing the linear.

The feminist psychoanalytic critics assert that the women should reconstruct the feminine to subvert the phallocentric oppression. They can relate the innocence of earlier state of their life with it. The age-old patriarchal dominance compels the women to restrain their language. Their self-opinion scarcely finds sufficient space for inner expression. The dominance of the patriarchal power structure forces Sujata to forget her language and communicate in an imposed discourse. When her husband Dibyanath denies her to take his car to Kanatapukur; she fails to resist against her husband's decision. She moves to Kantapukur without taking his car. Mother in her does not help to release from that psychological condition to assert her stand. Without explaining her side, she prefers to leave for the police morgue. It may be due to the fact that a wife is not allowed to challenge her husband's decision, conventionally. On the other hand, Indian English Drama has essentially a masculine structure. There is a little scope for women centred language in it. But existence of women lies particularly in their language. Until women start using their language; it will be difficult to have an expression of womanhood in their plays. In both the plays, *Bayen* and *Mother of 1084,* the experience of being a woman is class specific. The woman protagonists of these plays belong to different social classes but have similar or particular gender experience. Their gender becomes the cause of their suffering. They realize their subjectivity when their motherhood is challenged by the society. Catherine Thankamma (2002: 47-48) aptly puts:

> Through the portrayal of Chandidasi and Sujata, Mahasweta Devi projects the woman as Shakti—the

> embodiment of strength, and also one who is capable of boundless love. It is an interesting fact that Sita and Sati—the two archetypal quintessential figures of Indian womanhood are honoured for their loyalty and endurance but for their unique characteristics—dignity and a sense of self glossed over. It is this dignity that Mahasweta Devi's Sujata and Chandidasi project. Women have this power in spite of patriarchy; it may even be a by-product of patriarchy. However that may be it is this kind of positive reinforcement that women require to throw off the restraining shackles of the patriarchal system.

Sujata fails to find exact words to express her innermost feelings due to the lack of personal language. She hesitates to take any firm decision because she fails to develop the language of difference. But there should be a language of difference for an authentic expression. Sujata becomes habitual to follow the imposed language. That's why her interaction remains ineffective and under patriotic subsumption. The social values, ideals are male centred. Generally, man takes a decision and a woman is expected to follow it. There are a few occasions when a woman's decision becomes the family decision. Sujata Chatterjee's positive opinion about her son is that Brati does not carry any significance in the family. No attention is provided for her maternal affection and care for her son. Brati is a culprit for his father and siblings. Sujata could not support Brati out of her ignorance for Brati's work. She may be in a state that where ignorance is bliss, 'tis folly to be wise. Hence, she lacks the supportive language. Her ignorance is seen clearly when she informs Brati:

> How would you know? you never have time to read the papers, all that's going on in Calcutta! Young men from one locality aren't allowed these days to visit a different locality. They get killed if they do. (14)

In this way, Sujata finds the world of her interest proceeds further with it. Her decision resonates her capacity to response the inner urge. Being a mother, she desires to know for the first time her son and his engagements at least after his death. She conquers over 'lack' with the help of strangely aroused self will.

She shows faith in the dictum 'it is better to travel hopefully than to arrive'.

Had Sujata known Brati's mission, she would not have allowed him to leave home and meet his friends. There is certainly a mother's care in her language but a complete ignorance towards his outside activities. The male members in the family Dibyanath, Jyoti and Brati's sisters to some extent know very well about Brati's activities. Though Brati's sisters have not any important role in family matters; they are quite aware of Brati's ideological engagements. It is her ignorance that leaves Sujata to confess after Brati's death. At the same time, her ignorance insists to reveal the fact behind Brati's death. Lacanian term lack denotes the feeling of inferiority in an individual, arousing out of shame. Sujata considers herself inferior because like Somu's mother she could not understand her son's mission. Being a mother, she should have known everything about him. The anger for family members and also members of the society arouses particularly out of the feeling of repression. Her genuine feelings are repressed. There was not any importance in her family to what she thinks or wants. The repressed feelings find a way out only after her meeting with Somu's mother and Nandini. No one in the family likes Sujata's decision to visit them at least on her daughter, Tuli's, engagement day.

Julia Kristeva illustrates the difficulty of expressing the experience outside the range of her language accepted for interaction. The language for Sujata, Chandi, and Frieda's expression is not effective enough to elaborate their complete experience. The restrictions to the language are confronted particularly for limited scope of expression. Sujata fails to show her discomfort with the reaction of her family members after Brati's death. Her negligence towards husband's affair with a typist is a mute agreement with the situation. She accepts her subordinate position in the family and also in public affairs. Her silence is not her consent but her inability to play any kind of role. In this way, she is caught in the web of deficiency.

Sujata and Nandini meet and share the strategic difference in their life. Nandini, a young Marxist-Leninist, is bold enough to convey her ideological stand. She speaks out: "Money, jobs, and power didn't mean a thing to us. But there were the temptations that seduced those who had joined us only to betray us" (19). She does not think like a conventional woman who often fails to act according to inward feelings. Often, the patriarchy does not allow her to operate according to personal impulsions. Nandini mixes with male activists and shares their ideas. In this way, she has her own language—unprejudiced and authentic. She, like Sujata, does not struggle to find words to express her views. She has a crystal clear idea regarding her past. She mentions that "when we begin to suspect, and could analyze our past experiences, only then could we become more confident of our selves" (20). On the contrary, Sujata's failure to analyze her past leaves her in distress. She fails to learn from her past therefore could not construct her presesnt. Nandini illustrates the difference between the women of her generation and the women of Sujata's generation. She asserts: "You...my mother.... You all speak the same way (pause). You will never understand. You had never pladged everything you had to the cause of all, the way we had"! (20). Her radical views about the modern world relationship struck Sujata but definitely demonstrate her confident language. Nandini's language is her confidence, reality and frankness. She believes: "It's a deadly time when people do not belong to one other by virtue of kinship or ties of blood. Every one remains stranger these days to every one" (21). Nandini is the first woman to help Sujata to realize 'language of dependency'. She is one who inspires Sujata to take decision of her will. A woman requires another woman's help to come out from the complexities of life. As Urvashi helps Anuradha for self-realization in *Two Women,* similarly, Nandini helps Sujata in this regard. It is only after that a woman is able to constitute her gender experience. Nandini's firm stand, her language of confidence makes it easier for Sujata to come out from complexity and experience individuality. Nandini denies Sujata to visit her again on the basis of "what do you gain out of coming to me? You live with your past. I have to harness my present and think of the future" (26).

Sujata-Nandini relationship adds an important dimension to the play as far a relationship between two women is concerned. Sujata and Nandini look at the world with differing perspectives.

Nandini is Sujata's daughter's age but she is more mature and well aware of outside reality. She is conscious enough to know the fact that there is not any significant change in the socio-political condition even after Naxalite revolt. On the other hand, Sujata has a little knowledge of outside realities. Nandini helps her to realize that there is not any considerable change in the outside situation. The people around her have accepted a false reality. It is time to help people realize the truth. That's why the silence should be broken. The party scene is crucial in the play to demonstrate Sujata's liberation. Sujata Chatterjee, for the first time dares to communicate her innermost feelings to the men and women gathered for the party. She denies the patriarchal linguistic decoding and accepts her own language for expression. She prefers her language instead of symbolic discourse. She is capable enough to urge the people, gathered for the party, to take individual stance to look at the outside realities. She urges "Let this No of mine pierce the heart of this city, rise to the skies, be borne on the winds over the whole state to every nook and corner. ...Let's set the past, the preset, and future a tremble" (31). The transformation of Sujata is identified only after she acquires Semiotic, the language of self-realization. Her denial of dominated patriarchal discourse comes out in the form of her open refusal to accept the imposed social verdict. She disagrees to consider Brati's generation as a villain and custodian of law and order Saroj Pal as a hero. The strength she procures to deny the rulers helps her to reconstruct the self and subjectivity.

Mahasweta Devi juxtaposes in the play the contrasting images of two women of different generations. One represents the earlier generation of suppressed womanhood whereas the other young generation of liberated womanhood. The difference between them occurs particularly due to the way they look and accept their life. It is only after her meeting with Nandini, Sujata realizes her personal limitations and regrets for the restrictions in her life. She understands for the first time to herself and her son, Brati also. She responds while leaving Nandini's house: "Never mind. I'll find my way out" (27). The changed, confident language of Sujata illustrates her determination to liberate herself. Julia Kristeva blames that women are generally excluded from the representation frame. In most of the situations in life, they fail even to represent their individuality. Till, they do not represent, they are not individuals. Their individuality is their subjectivity. Sujata meets Nandini and helps to realize soft discrimination in her home that helps her to introspect her subjectivity. To the end of the play, Sujata urges loudly to men and women gathered for engagement party and symbolizes her realization. The party scene, in this way, becomes a paradigm of Sujata's unified voice for liberation. It is more psychological liberation that helps to come out of repression. She communicates her liberated self in a confident language.

> SUJATA: Did Brati die so you could carry on in your cadaverous existence, enjoying and indulging in all the images of the world, all the poetry, the red roses, the neon lamps...in his own happy happiness. (31)

It is an imposed recognition in Sujata's case that forces her natural joy to disappear. The imposed recognition does not allow her to free herself, easily. She strangles her personal happiness by agreeing to walk the conventional path blindly. She takes a great deal of time for realization. To the end of the play she commences her journey for the truth.

Sujata's role as a mother has a different connotation. Instead of social, she faces domestic restrictions. No one could realize her responsibilities towards Brati. That's why her appreciation for Brati is criticized almost all the time. In both the cases, negligence for a mother's role is at the forefront.

Both Sujata and Chandi are under the burden of their motherhood. Radha Chakravarthy (2008: 95) states clearly: "...the narrative of nationalism sought to create the abstract, homogenized figure of woman as mother to serve a particular political agenda, without any real concern for the needs of actual women in different sectors of the society."

Sujata Chatterjee decides to discover the reasons behind her son, Brati's death and in this way she journies from veil to vision to redefinie her own self and subjectivity. Realization and subjectivity help Sujata to determine future actions of her life. Julia Kristeva asserts the need of realization of subjectivity on woman's part to determine meaning in their lives. The realization becomes possible with the help of language. The change in Sujata's language is nothing but her decision to express according to personal concerns. There is a need of full, complete expression of woman's world of experience. Mahasweta Devi elaborates, in this way, a woman's transformation from dependency to independence in a male-dominated society.

The sense of being is predominant in the protagonists in these plays. The protagonists of these plays attempt, though considerably late in their life to redefine their self with the help of Semiotic. Liberation begins, in this way, with self-realization. Chandidasi in *Bayen* comes to a pragmatic realization that her service for the society is not appreciated. Hence, she determines to stop her work, choosen as a social responsibility. With a revolutionary spirit, she declares: "Go, I'll come and let the community know that this will be the last time that I'll do this job" (85). She denies the job of grave digging and keeping it not because she afraids to stay during nights but due to lack of social acknowledgement. No one comes forward to speak in her favour. Her honesty in performing social responsibilities stands unimportant for the lords like Gourdas. Hence, Chandi accumulates enough strength to communicate her disinterestedness. The symbolic male-centred order has not any scope for women. Mother, in patriarchal system is defined according to the notions of patriarchy. Woman receives marginal or no crux in this order. Chandi's longing to perform her duties as a mother is denied completely. Her sentiments are also not perceived by the society. The male-centred language dissociates a woman from the power structure. Women are discredited for their potentials also. Sujata's role in nurturing her children, her efforts in maintaining the home and abilities of an ideal wife are not credited to her because there is a lack of specific language to acknowledge her contribution.

In the plays of Mahasweta Devi, one comes across an association of women's oppression with the prominant social issues. She unearths the status of Indian woman in her social criticism. In this way, her treatment to the issues of women is radical and realistic. Chandi's oppression discloses her suffering in form of domestic and community discriminations. Her husband denies to take her side, amidst several difficulties in her life. Nobody comes out to save her from ostricization. The strange, uncomprehendible behaviour of Chandi is nothing but a psychic disorder. She loses her mental balance, to some extent and starts behaving in a strange manner. But unfortunately she is not understood by anybody of them. Mostly the behavioural difference causes the load of suppression. She is insulted now as a witch—'a woman who knows black magic'.

The language plays a vital role to suppress a woman's voice. It is crucial in the process of degrading a woman's status. Chandi receives abusing words, inferior language from her own people. The community curses her as a witch, a woman having evil powers. They hide their children to save them from her evil sight. Language, all the way becomes a medium to harm a woman's social status, in this way. Individuality of a woman causes a subconscious fear in the minds of patriarchal lords like Gourdas, the head of the village power structure. He receives constantly a threat to his rule with an emerging individuality in Chandi. She was brought up like a son by her father. Therefore, there is an inborn individuality in her personality. She does not feel any kind of fear to keep the graves during nights. Even after her marriage, she continues the work to satisfy her ancestors. In the absence of Chandi during nights, her husband Malinder does not take any step to perform mother's role. He insists her to keep graves during nights by reminding her ancestral duties. But fails to take any responsibility on his shoulders to look after their son. It is an outcome of patriarchal belief that woman should have a sense of mothering, naturally. She should take responsibility of children but at the same time should not fail in her outside responsibilities. He finds it as a simple way to avoid personal duties. The phallocentric assumptions compel Malinder to cold shoulder his responsibilities as a husband and also as a father.

The villainous mind of Gourdas dissociates Chandi from her duties. Gourdas and his men start using humiliating words for Chandi. It is to degrade her subjectivity. Chandi begins to loose her faith only after receiving these planned torments. To the end, Bhagirath accepts Chandi as his mother because he feels deeply the need of motherly compassion in his life. He speaks out in the midst of the fact that a woman's image has been restrained in the web of misogyny. She receives seldom words of praise from men and women. But Bhagirath's act of constituting her subjectivity is the matter of reconstruction of her image.

The way her community uses a discourse for Chandidasi in *Bayen* "You're a bayen" (86) shows the mentality of dominations. In a male-dominated society, it is habitual to degrade women and defame them as a bayen. In this way, language symbolizes the power. Chandi denies carrying further the load of ancestral responsibility. She feels deeply hurted for neglecting her efforts. She dares to deny the job. She shows an awareness regarding her subjectivity. Actually, it is in her denial, her subjectivity resists.

The society rarely shows any kind of concern for Chandi's motherhood as her ancestral responsibility is often emphasized. No one comes out to respect her motherhood. It is really unfortunate to have such an unacceptable dominating social tendency. A woman is expected to carry her social responsibilities forgetting quite easily her personal craving. The rethinking of subjectivity in Sujata's case (*Mother of 1084*) travels from subjugation to self-assertion. The subjugation she confronts is not class or race oriented but gender-centred. It is restricted to her subordinate position in domestic affairs. The way she has been considered and treated in her family shows her dependency. The self-assertion commences with her determination to investigate the reasons behind her son, Brati's death. Her journey, in this regard, changes her attitude diametrically. It helps to rethink subjectivity through self-realization.

Actually, the social structure denying any rights to women like Chandidasi is equal to Dystopia. The power structure does not ensure necessarily an authentic woman's experience. Therefore, it becomes essential to discover woman's authentic experience with the help of women-centred interpretations. Mahasweta Devi does not claim to be a feminist writer but explores it through signification and interpretation. She introspects the psychological shifts of her women characters and elaborates their status. Her attempt of reconstructing the value system highlights certainly her gender consideration. Bhagirath, to the end of play, accepts mother-son relationship openly. Bhagirath leads the way of reconstruction of social values by disclosing her identity. He shows thus his credence in the fact that when the things are at the worst, they begin to mend. Nancy Chodorow, a noted feminist scholar, acknowledges that a mother's role is always historically as well culturally specific in its organization, social meanings, and value. But it is not a realized fact in Chandi's case. There should have an acceptance of values that constitute mother of a woman. In this way, there are certain values as a mother in Chandi's personality. As her breasts start oozing, Chandi's longing for her son increases. But she is not allowed to feed her child or look after her needs.

The object relations theory explains how a child becomes a person. Bhagirath's act of accepting Chandi as his mother signifies his maturity. He becomes a person by showing his ability to take the decision of his choice. The theory also asserts that a mother herself helps the child to achieve a sense of self. The object-relations theory emphasizes child's mother and differs widely from the Freudian impression on oedipal conflict with each other. Object relations theory assists a child to accept separation and disillusion through various numbers responded to him. Bhagirath accepts virtually his separation from Chandi, his mother as his father and other members of the family fails to respond his passionate interrogations about his mother. A child faces a lot of trouble when his innate desire to meet his own mother remains unfulfilled. Bhagirath separates himself from his mother particularly out of his inability to meet her. But it is not a permanent separation. It takes some time for reunion. To the end of the play, Bhagirath comes out with a full spirit to reveal identity of his mother before his community. In both the plays, Mahasweta Devi explores self and subjectivity of women through oscillating attributes of motherhood whereas Manjula Padmanabhan discloses both positive and adverse aspects of women's discourse in her plays *Lights Out* and *Harvest.*

III

Manjula Padmanabhan, a well-known contemporary playwright, presents the world of bourgeoise men and women and their language in her highly acclaimed play *Lights Out*. Being a discussion play, *Lights Out* illustrates hypocrite tendency of middle-class individuals through their discussion. It is strange to experience their mean expression on a woman's molestation in a nearing compound of Bhaskar and Leela's flat. The frank, rude comments focus their adverse views on a woman's social position. Initially, Bhaskar tries excuses to avoid himself from calling police to stop the molestation of a woman.

LEELA : No one wants to do it alone. BHASKAR : Huh! So why should we!

LEELA : Because...because, I'm frightened! I can't bear it any more!

BHASKAR : Darling, what are you frightened of? Who would dare to hurt you? (140)

The comments of Bhaskar, his friends Mohan and Surrinder show their prejudiced views about women whereas Naina and Leela show their inability to take any firm stand to rescue the victim. The women characters fail to perform any meaningful action, signifying their individuality. Women in general confront difficulty in breaking the patriarchal restrictions and express themselves in an authentic way. Leela just goes on insisting her husband to call the police but she is unable to do anything in favour of the victim. Actually, the symbolic order in male-dominated society is not accessible to women. The fact is that women are prohibited to develop their own language for expression. The women generally communicate in an imposed speech. It causes the leading feminist critics like Julia Kristeva to develop women's linguistic structure. The present structure denies the symbolic order and aspires to construct a gender specific language in such a way that it would be a constant threat to the patriarchal symbolic order. A complete, woman-centred expression is possible through it. But there are not any signs of self-expression in Leela and Naina's stance.

As the play proceeds, the so-called sophisticated gentlemen and women prefer escapism. They pass on adverse remarks: "...A whore is not decent, so a whore cannot be raped!" (175). They assert, in this way, their attitude towards a woman's molestation. On the other hand, the women are present there to watch the brutal.

Leela comprises negligence to the semiotic aspect. The reaction to the molestation of a woman depicts the symbolic aspect. The patriarchal attitude is responsible to neglect the issues of women. Bhaskar, at last, finds a solution to stop their mind from thinking over the incident as he tries to release themselves from a woman's issue. He adds: "We'll just keep the window shut, draw the curtains and put on some music. In fact, why not put the music on right away..." (143).

It happens when women prefer the commonly accepted discourse. It does not allow them to show any concern for an outsider. There is not any kind of sympathy in Leela's speech. Being a woman, she should have bothered a woman's molestation. But she lacks certainly in demonstrating it. Her failure as a woman lies particularly in her inability to take any firm stand. Neither could she help the molested woman nor dissociate herself from unproductive discussions. Her mind in phallocentric society is prepared in such a way that there is not any scope for firm, confident set of mind. In patriarchal society, the language of violence is a sign relational of women's subordination.

Frieda's (an attendant) role in the play suggests her restricted, caged life. She is a mute witness of the discussion going on there. Frieda is not like other women characters in the play Naina and Leela, allowed to think beyond daily requirements. There is a language of dominated self in her mute, unquestioning behaviour. The playwright allows at the very outset to wonder what Frieda may be thinking throughout the play. Frieda in *Lights Out* does not utter a single word because she fails to obtain own's language. She struggles for the words out of her fear for communication. Her past might have damaged her language therefore she is mute, non-reactive. Frieda's silence suggests a woman's suppression in patriarchy. Frieda's silence throughout the play shows her failure in obtaining language of one's own. She is representative of millions of women who fail to response their subjectivity. On the other hand, the language of Leela and Naina does not express their subjectivity but shows their agreement with prejudiced male discourse.

Naina has a particular confused state of mind. Her disturbed mind fails to stop thinking about molestation against a woman in a nearing compound. It is a phenomenon among the middle-class women to keep themselves busy in gossiping the troubles of other women. They rarely trouble their minds to reach any solution or perform any meaningful action to rescue the victimized women from their difficulties. But there is a spark of individuality in Naina's expression and also an utter desire to help the victim. Actually, it is her difficulty to make her voice loud in front of her husband and other male members due to an accepted subordination.

The expression of self is possible only through an acceptance of individual's language denoting subjectivity. Consideration of subjectivity thus becomes the dominant mode of self-expression. The language of Leela and Naina could not be a medium of their self-expression because their expression is an utterance of male-dominated discourse. It is not so that they are anxious about a woman's molestation in the nearing compound. Particularly, Leela, enjoys it but cannot disclose openly like her husband. Leela's expression to the end of the play is quite crucial to know her hidden tendency. She mentions disappointedly: "Oh! Then it must be over for to night!" (189).

The play ends without any meaningful action. The so-called sophisticated men and women in the play fail to perform any action to stop the victimization of a helpless woman. In this way, Manjula Padmanabhan discloses the fact that subjectivity of a helpless, poor woman does not count any importance in Indian society. The brutal is mutely watched and senselessly reacted. On the other hand, the playwright illustrates a woman's complex appearance in modern society through Jaya's character in the play *Harvest*. She accepts without hesitation her immoral relationship with brother-in-law, Jitu. But at the same time, she fails to show any meaning to her being as a married woman. The renowned critics such as Kristeva, Irigary argue strongly the need of a meaningful self, formed particularly with the help of gender centred language. But Jaya's bold expression is not capable enough to explore her individuality, to a larger extent. Actually, "Resistance to the dominant at the level of the individual subject is the first stage in the production of alternative forms of the knowledge or where such alternatives already exist, of winning individuals over to these discourses and gradually increasing their social power" (Weedon: 111). Jaya fails substantially to form any personal significance. She is compelled to experience the torments in her family for being a woman only. She is not happy at all in her married life. Her husband fails considerably to fulfill her sexual desire. She desires the fulfillment in Jitu's company. But Jitu even prefers to play with her longing, her sexual desire. In this way, she remains an unsatisfied woman. There is not any proper consideration of her individuality by anybody in her family. Manjula Padmanabhan conveys here that how a woman's subordination troubles no one in Indian families. On the other hand, her mother-in-law goes on using humiliating words for Jaya. Their relation lacks affinity, concern and soft interaction. Ma comments: "I should have thrown her out from the moment she started making eyes at him..." (235). Ma being a woman should have tried to understand Jaya's suffering. But she could not stop herself from torturing Jaya for not having a child. Lack of a healthy, sound conversation between these two women, living under the same roof, is a postmodern reality. Emotional attachment is not a part of their relationship. Ma wastes most of her time in watching daily soaps and humiliating Jaya. She considers it as her birthright to degrade her daughter-in-law through all the possible ways. But, in course of time, Jaya attempts to define her personal significance. The feeling of individuality arises in her after bearing terrific mental torments. An individual's difference is impossible without language. Jaya and Ma certainly lack their own speech in the play. They communicate to humiliate dishonour each other only. Their speech is harmful and at the same time male centred. They interact usually in a harmful, vulgar language. Manjula Padmanabhan shows, in this way, the mode of woman's expression in the play.

Julia Kristeva explains that Semiotic illuminates the practice and process repressed by sign. In other words, it attempts to break the patriarchal restrains to express in an authentic way. Similarly, Jaya, to the concluding part of the play shows enough strength to defy the conventional discourse to form a concrete speech. She speaks out: "For the first time in my life and may be the last time of my life, I'm going to enjoy, myself, all by myself" (249). Her confident interaction is her ability to find a way out to her suppression in male-centred system. She is not more than a commodity for Om, Ma and Jitu. She strives for personal recognition and for the first time decides to express herself in a confident way.

The social common sense runs on the assumption that mother and child have an emotional attachment with each other. It sustains with biological stage shift. But the postmodern situation has replaced this assumption with a distressful fact that both mother and child have been dissociating from each other on the ground of emotional attachment. The relationship between Ma and Jitu is certainly a lesson in this regard. Neither Ma nor Jitu show any affection for each other. Ma does not hesitate to mention. "The gods left a jackal in my belly by mistake when they made him he's just like you (Jaya), rude, insolent, ungrateful..." (218). The way Ma looks at Jitu is certainly unbelievable.

Manjula Padmanbhan in both of her plays accentuates a different, a more radical aspect of woman's language. She does not present her women characters as Bharati Sarabhai and Mahasweta Devi have done in their plays. Though she shows her sympathy with Jaya and Frieda, she does not excuse Leela and Naina for their hypocritical attitude. She discloses both the aspects of a woman's nature through her women characters in the plays. As a playwright, she interrogates the lack of respect for a woman's subjectivity in our society. But at the same time, she does not deny the fact of having muffled way of thinking of so-called sophisticated women in our society.

IV

The women playwrights such as Bharati Sarabhai, Mahasweta Devi and Manjula Padmanabhan focus here on the fact that woman's authentic experience in other words is her voyage to 'mother's country'. These playwrights take their readers on the voyage to experience a world of liberated woman through the study of psychodynamics of language of their plays. Their thesis, in other words, is an attempt to have a replacement for the suppressed, unconcerned expression of women in male-dominated society. Woman's identity in our male-centred society does not go beyond her stereotyped image. But these women dramatists challenge the prejudiced construction of Indian woman by interrogating the issues such as woman's self and subjectivity. They connote it through a language that glorifies a woman's state of being a woman. They strive to take woman out of penis-envy and constitute a world of her experience by respecting her womanhood. Altogether, it is an attribution of woman's individuality denoting self-respect and social approval. The efforts to create the selfhood for women have considerably procured a reward in form of liberation of these women protagonists from phallocentric restrictions in the plays analyzed here. For example, Sujata visits Nandini's home on Tuli's engagement day ignoring disapproval of her family members. Chandi (*Bayen*) conveys her rejection of patriarchal responsibilities to her husband amidst her own limitations. It happens only after her realization of being a mother. Her realization proves to be a boost to encounter the difficulties in conventional patriarchal society. On the other hand, Jaya in *Harvest* and Naina in *Lights Out* speak at last in language of their own to challenge the decisions of their husbands. They show faith in inner voice and express themselves with a force. Old woman in *The Well of the People* and Anuradha in *Two Women* choose the similar path and show their ability in withstanding the barriers imposed on Indian women for centuries together. But at the same time, it should not be ignored that the women playwrights particularly Bharati Sarabhai and Mahasweta Devi fail to have a complete justice with changed perspectives of these women characters. To clarify the objection, I would like to mention the last scene in the play *Bayen* where a woman's identity gets an approval only after a male certifies it. It means even after her death Chandi could not free herself from the dominance of male-centred social setup. To some extent, Sujata, Old woman, and Anuradha have similar experience. Sujata could not dare to stop her husband from an immoral relation with a typist. Old woman fails to find words to response the nonsense of her mates after her decision to bulid a well for untouchables. To add further, Anuradha's state is not different. Even though her mate Urvashi compels her to take decision of her own choice; she fails to reciprocate. It happens due to the burden they have been carrying since their birth in androcentric society. Apart from these limitations, the contribution of these playwrights in making the voice of women characters more solid, confident, and authentic is noteworthy. Certainly, they lead the way of woman-centred world with an utmost pride and strength.

References

Chakravarthy, Radha (2008). *Feminism and Contemporary Women Writers: Rethinking Subjectivity.* New York: Routledge.

Devi, Mahasweta. (1997). *Five Plays.* Calcutta: Seagull Books.

Gilbert, Helen (Ed.) (2001). *Postcolonial Plays: An Anthology.* New York: Routledge.

Padmanabhan, Manjula (1997). *Lights Out.* Calcutta: Seagull Books.

______ (2001). *Harvest.* In Helen Gilbert (Ed.): 217-49.

Sarabhai, Bharati (1942). *The Well of the People.* Calcutta: Vishwa Bharati.

______ (1950). *Two Women.* Bombay: Hind Kitabs Pvt. Ltd.

Spender, Dale (2011). *Man Made Language* cited in Peter Berry. *Beginning Theory.* Mumbai: Viva Books.

Thankamma, Catherine (2002). "The Women Patriarchy Created: A Study of the Plays of Vijay Tendulkar, Mahesh Dattani and Mahasweta Devi." *Theatre India.* (40):2 (May): 42-48.

Weedon, Chris (1987). *Feminist Practice and Post-Structuralist Theory.* Cambridge MA and Oxford UK: Blackwell.

4
Staging Womanhood

> The female body is not reducible to a sign free of connotation. Women always bear the mark and meaning of their sex which inscribes them within cultural hierarchy.
>
> —Jill Dolan

The present chapter illustrates the dramatic techniques in the selected plays of Bharati Sarabhai, Mahasweta Devi and Manjula Padmanabhan. Though women's theatre in India is a marginal entity; the strategic merits of these women playwrights certainly deserve a mention. The contemporary women playwrights such as Manjula Padmanabhan, Poile Sengupta are with time as far their stage skills concerned. With a skillful dramaturgy these playwrights have gained a respective position in the world of theatre. Their stage covers the different saspects interrogating woman's position in the power structure. The central aspect here is to focus the innovative stage devices in their plays.

I

Bharati Sarabhai's *The Well of the People* celebrates 'the pleasure of the text' of Roland Barthes. The playwright takes her liberty of writing and so the reader of its reading. The poetic narration does not follow necessarily the conventional pattern. It creates certainly the music, rhyming essence; one of the characteristic requirements of a poetic play but at the same time offers a change in the conventional pattern at certain places. The playwright does not regret for this changed pattern because she accepts it as an experiment. It is not certainly an arbitrary subversion but a significant experimentation. The play, possibly as in deconstruction method, scrutinizes and displaces the traditional formation annihilating them completely. But at most of the places, the heavy dose of poetic complexity, in pursuit of a new, troubles readers' mind. It would have been possible for the playwright to denote the idea in a simple way for the realization of the reader or viewer but the playwright fails to do it considerably. She merges the Western and Indian theatrical conventions at many places in the play.

W.B. Yeats, the proponent of Poetic Drama considers his Abbey Theatre as a true 'People's Theatre' and states further:

> ...the first doing of something for which the world is ripe, something that will be done all over the world and done more perfectly; the making articulate of all the dumb classes each with its own knowledge of the world, its own dignity but all objective with the objectivity of the office and the workshop of the newspaper and the street, of mechanism and of politics. (Bentley: 331)

Similarly, Bharati Sarabhai's *The Well of the People* becomes the voice of millions of dumb Indians who have lost their voice under the British rule. They are unable to fight for their rights. The play is crucial for its spatial essence because the subjects of her play like plight of the old woman, inhumanity with peasants and workers, Gandhi's arrival on political scene are incorporated in such a way that they help to discover the element of social realism in it.

The play had hardly been performed anywhere. It seems as the playwright was more careful to present it as a text rather its performance merits. But if one thinks about its performance; it is certainly challenging out of the six focus points, Aristotle had suggested. The play certainly differentiates on the basis of Dianoia it creates and the Melos, sweetens to our ears. To some extent, "Bharati Sarabhai's attempt to capture the soul of India; as a work of art, the play succeeds but as theatre it fails to lack of that infrastructure which is necessary for the successful communication of the play" (Joshi: 14).

The chorus, formed on both sides of the stage, discloses the story of the old woman with a beautiful poetic knotting throughout the play. As T.S. Eliot comments 'poetry is the third voice in the theatre', similarly the use of poetry becomes the major performing tool. The Gandhian chorus explains the earlier unsuccessful attempts of old woman to reach Haridwar. Yet her zeal to fulfill the dream cannot be withdrawn easily from her being. Chetan, a young Gandhian worker fails to cope with the fact that Indians have such an indomitable passion for pilgrimage. They are eager to reach there at least once in their life. Hence, it becomes difficult for the followers like him to carry forward the message of spiritual idealism, successfully. On the other hand, a skillful narration is strength of the play. The narration runs thus:

> Countrywide the devout have come, carried their large families, wives with sprightly wits and small, hidden babies and soft glossy spirits.
>
> The sacred river has become a bed for all, enough a bundle and pitcher. (11)

The shift from present to previous is as effective as the flashback technique in the movies. With a coherence, the playwright moves backward and forward throughout the play. The two groups of chorus are not mere groups but two different worlds exactly, i.e. the world of reality and the world of dramatic illusion. It can be equated with Augusto Boal's Theatre of the Oppressed where we meet reality and illusion, simultaneously. The play also follows the footsteps of classical theatre with its poetic quintessence. It is a modest endeavour on the part of playwright to restore our age-old theatrical miracle. The play assimilates also with Epic Theatre, one of the crucial modern schools of theatre, as far its concern for social realism. Bharati Sarabhai's effort to deal with it in a poetic style is the sole example of its kind. In this way, Pablo Neruda's observation that 'Theatre is not poetry, it can't be done in seclusion, it is the most public of the art forms and has to reach out to the masses' definitely goes wrong.

The shift is interchangeable. There is not any clearly demonstrated difference or separation of one from the other. We reach to a workroom of the volunteers. The playwright states the shift in the narration itself. It gives a picture of typical Indian villagehood. The volunteers like Chetan, Vichitra and Sanatan have an immense faith in Gandhian ideals. They have been working with devotion in old woman's village to persuade for a change in the lives of these poor villagers. The volunteers are mediators between Mahatma Gandhi and the village folk. The infinite message of genuine spiritualism is to be spread among the villagers. The conventional faith of these people was not challenged earlier by anybody. Any kind of change is difficult to accept when it damages earlier faith. The ardent volunteers accept the challenge and work in a signified direction. They ought to buoy up the villagers to unite against the British rule. The chorus of peasants formulates a decisive position in the play. It represents the millions of Indians who had been suffering severely under British tyranny. The poor farmers and peasants were not in position at all to remember the day when they were extremely happy.

The comprising of two groups on the two sides remains perfectly compatible with street theatre type. The chorus of peasants comments on difficulties they have been facing under the British and Sahukar raj in Indian villages. They lag considerably behind to ensure the pleasures of life. One of the peasants comments:

> And new usurer of our age, the British
> Trader, collector, administrator
> On top of the old village arbitrator. (25)

It is rather an arduous experience for a researcher to percept perfectly the poetic coherence in this part of the play. Monika Verma boldly comments in her critique on this play. "The whole of *The Well of the People* is full of 'feeling'. In fact the writer 'feels' so much that she cannot express herself coherently." The first peasant in the chorus comments:

> We have heard of a tree.
> It has no trunk, no branch.
> It is one face,
> All lotus. (35)

Monika Varma objects strongly the use of obscure verses in the play. She considers this overdose of poetry as 'witch's brew'. She fears for disappearance of original meaning due to complex poetry. She mentions further 'piling up of words, unreal'. In this way, Monika Varma advocates simplification of the subject to make the central idea quite clear for the readers. There should not be any specific language of the literature when the day-to-day dialect is enough to serve the purpose.

The shift from village scene to Haridwar scene and vice versa is significant to emphasize the main theme. The playwright has done it frequently throughout the play. Her excellence lies in doing it with a greater effect. The playwright does not follow blindly Yeatsian or Eliotian pattern as far her poetic expression is concerned. She, rather Indianizes the Western poetic devices for an effective presentation. Her poetic experiment matches considerably with Eliot's similar attempt in his celebrated play *Murder in the Cathedral.* Bharati Sarabhai makes her play purposely a simple and actable version with a prior consideration to its subject. An absolute co-ordination between the theme and its form is strength of the play. There is certainly inevitability between these two elements. Though the play follows footsteps of Augusto Boal's Theatre of the Oppressed and its offspring Street Theatre, to some extent, the playwright takes her liberty to make certain changes in its presentation. On the other hand, the old woman in the play undertakes different positions at one and the same time. The playwright observes: "...the India with not only her jewels taken from her but her land, her food, her heroic children, to be used in the service of an alien people imposing their will on her" (05). All together, the versical attempt of Bharati Sarabhai captures reader and viewer for its fusion of contrasting presentation methods.

The other play, *Two Women,* is an Indian subject presented in accordance with Western and particularly in Eliotian style, to some extent. The play demonstrates effectively Bharati Sarabhai's indominatable zeal to execute the Western style to handle a typical Indian subject. The play is an example of a vibrant and audible dramatic expression during pre-Independence phase of Indian English Drama. The play is crucial for its skilled stylization.

Almost all the scenes in the play take place in Kanak Raya's sitting room. Though there is a scope to raise the negligence of Unity of Time in the play. Bharati Sarabhai does not miss to match the background with the action, taking place on the stage. The drawing room of Kanak Raya is divided into two parts. The division of room in two parts signifies a difference in attitude. Kanak Raya's part is decorated typically in Western style to show his innermost passion for the Western culture. His anglicized style of living is reflected through the way the left part of the room is adorned. This part of the room is with glittering steel furniture. The ornamental book cases are really attractive. In every possible way the left part is made attractive and modern in its appearance. On the other hand, the right part of the room is typically Indian and chairs, made of Indian wood are arranged carefully for sitting purpose. Anuradha's Krishna Bhakti is shown through the potrayal of Shri Krishna, hanging on the wall. All together, the drawing room is clean, polished and well-decorated. It captivates certainly a visitor's attention. Bharati Sarabhai maintains a balance to present these contrasting parts of the room. She states symbolically the cultural conflict. Indian rich class, after Independence of the nation, could not give up its fascination for the Western style. Kanak's part is representative of this fascination whereas Anuradha's part represents conventional Indian style. In other words, it is a depiction of accidental-oriental culture conflict. The characters in the play are indirectly divided as per their personal interests. Anuradha, Urvashi Devi and Lata form a group on the basis of their captivation for conventionalism. They are typically Indianized in their appearance and behaviour. Kanak Raya, Miss Boulton and Sudha whereas have a concern for Western lifestyle. To a greater extent, an indirect division of characters in two groups gives an impression of cultural conflict to the present subject.

Anuradha's part 'a Radha's Corner', i.e. half-part of Kanak's sitting room is disliked by Kanak. Without any hesitation, he conveys his adverse views: "You have not has a proper education.

You are taken it with flimsy arguments, a little flashness" (15). He also adds: "Not that I have anything against your patronizing home-made products. Quite good in their own way, but don't go so far as to patronize home-made ideas" (*ibid.*). In this way, Kanak Raya asserts his preference for the Western style by criticizing his wife's faith in conventional lifestyle.

The third act in the play testifies Bharati Sarabhai's handling of the stage devices and making her presentation more effective. She personifies Himalaya here to depict Anuradha's deep-rooted longing to stay at Himalaya for remaining part of her life. It is an example of Bharati Sarabhai's outstanding dramatic craft that makes her audience to praise her efforts. An off-stage voice, "I am here" (94) signifies Anuradha's anxiety to visit the Himalayan abode. Sarabhai shows the inward Himalaya in Anuradha's consciousness with its outside physical form. Sarabhai displays it in such way that one feels Himalaya is communicating with Anuradha.

VOICE : Himalaya!
CHANT : Himalaya!
VOICE : You seek me.
CHANT : You seek me.
...
VOICE : Himalaya is here.
CHANT : Himalaya is here. (94)

The playwright succeeds in doing it with the help of lights on the stage. Resonance of sound illustrates Anuradha's longing to fulfill her dream. The playwright uses effectively 'Voice' to explore an utter desire of her protagonist. The playwright maintains it by showing the picture of Himalaya. On the other hand, the moonlight on the stage is again an example of Sarabhai's excellent stage handling. To conclude, Bharati Sarabhai handles two different forms in her plays. *The Well of the People* is a versical type while *Two Women* is a prose type. But in both of her plays there are a number of places where her dramatic strategy surpasses her contemporaries, to a great extent. On the other hand, it is definitely incredible to see a woman playwright is handling the stage with such an ease. Sarabhai's technicality differs from Mahasweta Devi on the basis of simple presentation. Mahasweta Devi makes her presentation considerably easy as she intends to demonstrate the world of neglected people.

II

The theatre of Mahasweta Devi is popular for oppressed, marginalized community. Her theatrical engagements show her intimate association with Augusto Boal's Theatre of the Oppressed. Boal has suggested that "...the theatre of the bourgeoisie is a finished theatre in which images of a complete and perfect world are presented. But since the oppressed classes do not know what their world would be like their theatre is unfinished—so there theatre is—a rehearsal for revolution" (Srampikal: 28). Similarly, Mahasweta Devi's theatre is an unfinished one because it believes in presenting the real life of subalterns. The stage strategies are often crucial to percept the ideas in the plays of Mahasweta Devi. She maintains stage economy throughout her presentation. The meagre stage prop undermines her intention and the actual presentation.

The play *Mother of 1084* enacts a day in the protagonist, Sujata Chatterjee's life, a day after two years of her son's death. She set to discover the causes behind Brati's death. The play has a firm dramatic structure with a beginning, middle and an end. It is one of the prominent plays of Mahasweta Devi where the structural standard is maintained to elaborate a comprehensive meaning. The playwright goes on making certain shifts from present to past and *vice versa* to develop the subject of her play. The play begins with the news of Brati's death. In this way, the play begins from middle that continues till fourth scene in the play. The scenes number fifth, sixth and seventh are about Brati's mission and his death in a mob attack. The stage of Mahasweta Devi is remarkable for its simple but meaningful devices. Talking about her stage, E. Satyanarayana (2000: 32) comments: "The stage is free of superfluous theatrical properties which give the playwright great freedom to present different situations more by suggestion than by scenic displays without taxing more the belief of the audience."

As Mahasweta Devi implements moderate prop on the stage, the use of lights therefore becomes significant. The shift from earlier to later scene is shown with the help of partial stage darkening. It is cleverly done to the end of fourth scene in the play. We shift now from present to past incident and hear a dialogue between Sujata and Brati. In this way, a simple use of lights helps for a crucial shift. It is again to the end of seventh scene as the eighth scene opens with a conversation between Sujata and Somu's mother.

The use of tape-recorder as a stage device becomes one of the dominant aspects of the play. The tape is used for soliloquy. Sujata's voice on the tape is a kind of soliloquy. It goes thus: "I went to Somu's mother in the afternoon. One can now visit the colony. There's no disturbance any more, no terror, no sirens, no gunshots, no screaming young men—no! (Pause). It was the second time I visited Somu's mother (Pause). I didn't know Brati well enough, Somu's mother knew him better" (9). The audience is helped here to percept Sujata's inward feelings. The most significant use of tape-recorder takes place just before Sujata's address to men and women gathered for the party. All the way, the technicality of *Mother of 1084* suggests Mahasweta Devi's credence in simple, common devices explaining a wider, crucial meaning and they explore also the mind of her characters.

Mother of 1084 surprisingly resembles the use of 'Stream of Consciousness' technique in the novels. In its novel form, there is a clear cut inclination for it whereas in drama form, it is done with a skillful use of tape-recorder. The instrument thus becomes *modus operandi* as Sujata determines her next action in accordance to earlier. The particular day (day of action) from dawn to night has contrasting actions. These actions are communicated through tape-recorder. All the way, the stage device is poignant to determine Sujata's mindset.

The technical standard of *Mother of 1084* relies largely on the way Mahasweta Devi maintains a balance between past and present events. On the other hand, *Bayen* is again a paradigm of Mahasweta Devi's theatrical economy.

In *Bayen*, Mahasweta Devi deals with gestures as a part of her theatrical economy. The gestures are quite significant in Brechtian and Boal theatre. In Augusto Boal's Theatre of the Oppressed particularly, the performance reaches to pinnacle with the help of meaningful gestures of the characters. The gestures serve the determined purpose of the actor without any decorative, sublime or expensive prop. Badal Sircar, the proponent of Third Theatre in India modeled most of his plays on the similar performance tricks which helped to propagate the subaltern issues in a simple but effective way. Likewise, Mahasweta Devi, an activist writer, emphasizes the issues related to the plight of underdogs with the help of simple dramatic techniques. The stage strategy of Mahasweta Devi demonstrates her attitude of theatrical economy. She aspires to propagate a boarder meaning with the help of limited and inexpensive stage devices in both the plays for present study is authenticated with a spatial essence. The simple stage devices help immensely for effective and accurate performance. Apart from this, Mahasweta Devi becomes an effective medium to reach people with an indominatable concern to explore social reality. Malinder, the male protagonist in the play, goes twelve year back by rearranging his hair and dhoti. With the help of effective gestures, he narrates the incident before his son:

> Hey, king, you have things to give to all those who never cared for you when you were in misery.
>
> I gave you food then, I gave you clothes. What have you for me? Eh?
>
> We are Gangaputtas. What are you going to give to our clan?... What you have for us?
>
> For my community?
>
> The Brahamins, the sadhus, the sanyasi get cattle, land and gold, and we get all the cremation grounds of the world.
>
> All the cremation grounds of the world for us, for us, for us, for us only. (78-79)

Malinder narrates the events in such a way to make it a live action. The gestures help to present the past incident in a more effective way. Malinder also narrates his romance with Chandi and their marriage, following it. Mahasweta Devi uses a tribal song here with a grace.

> ...Drunk with colour, Our bodies too are drunk.
>
> The heart's too full of colour, Let the colour spill over the body Let the colour flow all over. (80)

Her stage strategy goes hand in hand with her subject. Mahasweta Devi, in both of her plays, elaborates the subject and makes an effective presentation with the help of her stage strategy. With simple, ordinary devices, she creates a magnificent impression. On the other hand, Manjula Padmanabhan implements modern technological devices to makes her presentation relevant to the subject of her plays.

III

The feminist *avant-garde* theatre is known particularly for its non-linear dramatic form. It argues, in this way, a break from the conventional theatrical strategies. Being one of the leading contemporary Indian English dramatists, Manjula Padmanabhan's dramatic caliber is particularly in her ability to develop her theatre as a non-linear entity. Her plays *Lights Out* and *Harvest* occupy a respective position in the firmament of Indian English Drama for their unconventional formation. As a playwright, Manjula Padmanabhan does not lag behind her male counterparts as far theatrical experimentation is concerned. The new media input, projection of advanced devices give a different theatrical experience to the audience while speculating her plays. In both of her plays, she uses modern technological devices to reach her audience by keeping the effect at the highest position.

The use of Brechtian theatre apparatus' in *Lights Out* makes a proficient presentation. These apparatus' help to deal with the issues of women with a greater significance. Elin Diamond (1988: 91) argues that "(a) gestic feminist criticism would 'alienate' or foreground those moments in a play text in which social attitudes about gender could be made visible." The social gestus of Brecht is instrumental, in this way, to reveal the gender discrimination under patriarchal system. Brecht's social gestus allows the playwrights to use the property that can make the presentation documentary in its form. Patrice Pavis (1982: 45) has aptly described the term Gestus in her observations on Brecht's Gestus. She illustrates:

> Instead of fusing logos and gestuality in an illusion of reality, the *Gestus* radically cleaves the performance into two blocks: the shown (the said) and the showing (the saying). Discourse no longer has the form of a homogeneous block; it threatens at any moment to break away from its enunciator. Far from assuring the construction and the continuity of the action, it intervenes to stop the movement and to comment on what might have been acted on the stage. *Gestus* thus displaces the dialectic between ideas and actions; the dialectic no longer operates within the system of these ideas and actions, but at the point of interaction of the enunciating gesture and the enunciated discourse.

The Brechtian gestus thus demonstrates physical gesture to define a character on the stage. The loud cry of the woman seeking help symbolizes a woman's oppression in a male-dominated society. Her loud cry becomes a metaphor of her suffering in phallocentric system.

There is a contrasting gesture to this loud sound. It is Frieda's meaningful silence. She does not utter a single word. But her physical gesture is enough to guess the working of her mind. While introducing Frieda, the playwright clears: "She remains constantly in sight, performing her duties in a mute, undemanding way.... The audience should be allowed to wonder what she thinks" (34). Frieda's silence is a metaphor of long back muteness of woman under male dominance. There are two contrasting ways of reaction of two different women but male domination is at the centre of both of them.

The stage décor is significant in *Lights Out*. Leela and Bhaskar's flat is decorated in an extremely attractive manner. But there is a strategy behind concentrating this external decoration. It is particularly to display middle-class show-off mentality as Leela spends most of her time and money in external decoration.

The use of light and screen shows Manjula Padmanabhan's strong inclination for modern devices. On the screen, important information about the play is displayed. It gives, in this way, the details of the incident on which the play is based.

The Brechtian technique helps rethinking of artistic self in *Lights Out*. The self of a woman becomes more unquenched. For example, the use of projector is appropriate and relevant in *Lights Out* to comprehend the inner feelings. Screaming of a woman signifies the gender oppression. Frieda's silence in the play signifies gest for suppression. A woman loses her tongue due to social suppression. The window is not opened in the play to signify the negligence of the society towards violence against a woman.

The interior decoration of Leela and Bhaskar's flat signifies their upper middle class stature. Leela might have taken a great deal of interest in decorating the flat with an intention to show their wealth. It is decorated with all the required decorative materials to make it more attractive. The lighting, floor, and ceiling décor give an impressive feel to the visitors. The interior decoration emphasizes typical middle-class flat culture.

Manjula Padmanabhan uses lights as a significant stage device. Padmanabhan's ability to use lights as a meaningful gestus can be seen clearly in the play. The lights help to catch different reactions on men and women, discussing a 'woman's molestation'. Mostly facial expressions are quite sufficient to encapsulate the inner working. In this way, the use of lighting becomes a crucial stage prop in the play.

Besides, the crafty handling of screaming coming from window side helps to maintain integrity of the subject. It becomes a Brechtian gestus that communicates a woman's struggle to free herself from sexual oppression. Bhaskar's bourgeois mind decides to switch on the cassette player to mask the sound. His attempt to suppress the outside sound shows his escapism.

Helen Gilbert (2001: 216) aptly puts her views on Manjula Padmanabhan's this award-winning play. She states: "*Harvest*'s bitter narrative is driven by a utopian impulse to suggest impossible possibility of a world in which there are no winners or losers, only partners." Manjula Padmanabhan has signified the essence of the play with the help of crafty theatrical devices. The implementation of modern technological apparatus is certainly meaningful here. Being a leading contemporary playwright, Manjula Padmanabhan denotes her trust in these devices for an impressive presentation. Her techno-savvy attitude helps certainly for a direct appeal to her audience.

Ginny, an agent of Interplanta appears before Om's family through a moduler. Her appearance is indicated as "The working tone sounds, the CONTACT MODULE lights up" (228). The warning bell leaves Om's family to fright. Symbolically, it is the way how Third-World people are governed by the First-World dominators. In this way, the warning bell becomes a powerful instrument to indicate the power of the First World. The dramatic excellence of Padmanabhan is particularly in her effective presentation of Ginny through a contact module. Actually, drama demands a direct, physical presence of its character. But instead of presenting Ginny on the stage, she takes help of these gadgets to make her presentation effective. Padmanabhan shows, in this way, her friendliness with modern technology and gives a new performance technique to Indian theatre. Manjula Padmanabhan has used gestures in her play, *Lights Out* on Brechtian social gestus model. Similarly, there is use of gestures in *Harvest* for a meaningful purpose. The gestures in the play help to demonstrate inner working of her characters. Particularly, Jaya, Jitu and Virgil's gestures are significant in the play. Jaya's complexity, anxiety and sorrow, these different aspects of her mood have been illustrated through meaningful gestures. These gestures help to perceive difficulties in Jaya's personal life. Her dissatisfied married life is presented through these meaningful gestures. On the other hand, Jitu, converted as Virgil signifies the difference, accurately. Manjula Padmanabhan's skillful handling makes it a remarkable shift.

The stage changes with the scenes in the present play. In the first scene of the first act, the playwright succeeds in creating city-life background. It is created here through the sounds of inner city traffic. The playwright uses lights effectively to focus the location. In this way, Manjula Padmanabhan, from the very beginning shows her concern for stage devices and proves her skilled efforts in doing it. As one proceeds to second scene in the first act, the sitting room of Om's house is slightly changed. As all of scenes in *Lights Out* take place in sitting room, similarly all the scenes in *Harvest* take place in Om's sitting room. The narration in the beginning of the scene goes thus: "There are brightly coloured instruction leaflets, elaborately devised containers for pills and powders and a number of small gadgets similar in size and shap to a slide-viewing device but of obscure purpose" (222). The third scene in the first act is a night scene. The playwright uses shadowy figures to signify Jaya's movements.

The playwright takes space between two acts in the play. The sitting room of Omprakash is decorated now with costly gadgets. One sees TV set, computer terminal mini gym, and air conditioner in this small room. The conversion of simple sitting room of Om's house into a well decorated room with costly gadgets indicates a complete change in personal life of Om and his family members. There are all the comforts at their disposal, now.

The second scene in the second act depicts the changed life style of Om's family. The third and forth scene of the same act continue with the similar preference. The playwright highlights these swift changes in Om's external life with a considerable measure of success.

The first scene in the third act of the play shows: "Ma is watching TV, wearing head-phones" (238). The changed, materialistic lifestyle is meaningful here. It signifies a change in external behaviour of the characters. The contact module, fitted in the sitting room with a web camera becomes a dominating role player in this part of the play. It starts governing the activities of the organ donator, Omprakash. A machine controls his life, to a great extent.

Manjula Padmanabhan illustrates the different emotional stages such as gloom, enjoyment and confession in Om's family with the help of specific stage devices. The play *Harvest* becomes an example of Padmanabhan's theatrical *magnum opus*, in this way.

IV

The stage strategy in the plays of these three playwrights illuminates inclination of women playwrights to use woman's body to explore the diverse aspects related to woman's socio-cultural construction. As Helen Cixous (1976: 879) has rightly stated: "women must write through their bodies, they must invent the impregnable language that will wreck partitions, classes and rhetorics, regulations and codes, they must submerge, cut through, get beyond the ultimate reserve discourse, including the one that laugh at the very idea of pronouncing the word silence...." The use of woman's body on the stage containing her gestures, movements and language certainly shows woman's ability to convey a wide range of experiences related to her subjectivity.

References

Cixous, Helen (1976). "The Laugh of the Medusa." *Signs*. The University of Chicago Press. 1:4 (Summer): 875-93.

Devi, Mahasweta (1997). *Five Plays*. Trans. Samik Bandyopadhyay. Calcutta: Seagull Books.

Diamond, Elin (1988). "Brechtian Theory/Feminist Theory: Toward a Gestic Feminist Criticism." *The Drama Review*. 32:1 (Spring): 82-94.

Eric, Bentley (1989). *The Theory of Modern Stage: An Introduction to Modern Theatre and Drama*. New York: Penguin Books.

Gilbert, Helen (Ed.) (2001). *Postcolonial Plays: An Anthology*. New York: Routledge.

Joshi, R.G. (1997). *Myth in Indian Drama*. New Delhi: B.R. Publishing Corporation.

Pavis, Patrica (1982). *Language of the Stage: Essays in the Semiology of the Theatre*. New York: PAJ Publications.

Padmanabhan, Manjula. (1997). *Lights Out*. Included in *City Plays*. New Delhi: Seagull Books: 135-90.

_____ (2001). *Harvest*. In Helen Gilbert (Ed.): 217-49.

Sarabhai, Bharati (1943). *The Well of the People*. Calcutta: Vishva-Bharati.

_____ (1952). *Two Women*. Mumbai: Hind Kitabs Ltd.

Srampickal, Jacob (1994). *Voice to the Voiceless: The Power of People's Theatre in India*. London: Hurst and Company.

Varma, Monika (1973). "Bharati Sarabhai." *Facing Four*. Calcutta: Writers Workshop: 35-42.

Yeats, W.B. (1989). "People's Theatre". In Bentley, Eric: 327-39.

5

Conclusion

> One good that has come of this commercial success, in addition to whatever fame and fortune has accrued for the writers, actors, producers, directors, and other theatre personnel and investors, is that it has called into question the qualities crucial to an authentic feminist theatre.
>
> —Helen Keysser

The previous chapters interweave a tangible link among the distinct aspects exploring woman's self and subjectivity in a male-dominated society in the plays of Bharati Sarabhai, Mahasweta Devi and Manjula Padmanabhan. The psycho-feminist aspect ascertains the loss of language, the gender perspective asserts socio-cultural subordination of a woman whereas the stage strategy emphasizes the prolonged desire to differentiate woman from the dominant dramatic tradition. In this way, the plays unearth the world of women encountering the challenges on the basis of mind, body and action. The book resonates the experience of women that helps to shape woman's worldview, a better perception of outside realities and a distinct tradition aspiring to get roots like the dominant male dramatic tradition in India. The present chapter summarises the arguments made in the earlier chapters and elaborates further the findings.

I

The dramatic tradition has been rooted in classical Sanskrit theatre. It is *fons et origo* of Indian drama. Bharatmuni's *Natyashastra*, a text on dramaturgy is the first ever book in the history of Indian drama giving an exhaustive guideline regarding writing and performance of a drama text. In this way, the *magnum opus* becomes a pioneering text on Indian dramaturgy. Actually, the classical Sanskrit drama was a product of strenuous efforts of playwrights such as Bhasa, Kalidasa, Bhavabhuti, Vishakhadatta and Sudraka. These playwrights were responsible for a glorious male dramatic tradition in India. But, on the other hand, Indian woman could get a marginal importance in socio-cultural Indian life for centuries. Actually, the plays fortified the male-centred socio-cultural conceptions and considerably neglected woman's social stature. It resulted into a scanty involvement of women writers in the field of drama. The issues related to woman's life and her overall experience could not find any respectable position in Indian plays for a long time. It might have not realized that a woman has also a decent position in the society. She is equally significant in power structure. Besides, women themselves could not write any play or dream its performance. In this way, the classical Sanskrit dramatic tradition disregarded the importance of woman for an ideal social life.

The classical theatre began wanning after an emergence of folk theatre in different parts of the country. Like Sanskrit drama, the present dramatic form attempted to reinforce male dramatic tradition. It is observed that "...all indigenous forms that predate colonialism or lie outside the spheres of European norms are valorized as natural, organic, and transcendent" (Dharwadkar: 310). The folk performances played a vital role in putting male dominance on dramaturgy. The overall picture was not encouraging for women writers in India to opt drama as a mode of their literary expression. On the other hand, the issues of women's personal and social being could receive a slight representation in these performances. As classical theatre had marginally presented women's issues; the folk performances also gave a little significance to represent woman's life in theatre. The dissolute life of women in patriarchal society could not be the subject of these performances. These performances were mainly aimed at entertaining the people from different walks of life. The stereotyped image of woman in these performances was restricted either to amuse or grant an apotheosis stature. She was rarely treated as a woman. The difficulties of an ordinary woman could not find any significant place in these performances. To some extent, Badal Sircar, one of the proponents of 'The New Theatre' in India showed his concern for the predicament of Indian woman in his plays. Altogether, the folk theatrical tradition in India could not enact substantially Indian woman's individual as well as social life through the performances. In this way, it continued the dominant-male tradition to a great extent. Actually, "Theatre is essentially—almost by definition—a public, social and hence male-dominated art" (Shepherd and Wallis: 70). Therefore, the dominance of men over the different segments of drama cannot be neglected. It is stated further "The dominant public action both on stage and in the audience stresses a male world in which women are either kept to the sides, in recesses, or are placed on display for the male viewer" (*ibid.*: 71). The dominant dramatic tradition till folk theatre in India discloses the similar fact. The representation of womanhood in drama has been dominantly a male-centred perspective. Firstly, there was a marginal scope to reveal self through the dramatic performance. Next, there was rarely a viable speech for her communication. The patriarchal domination gave fewer opportunities to interact the different aspects of womanhood. It showed the way a woman's image is being constructed in course of history. The interpretations of her image mostly feature a subordinated treatment to her biological presence.

On the other hand, the female dramatic tradition in India is not as rooted as the predominant male tradition. The women writers in India show considerably little interest in the field of drama. The art of drama is among the five Vedas in ancient culture in India. It is a part of India's glorious heritage. But the women writers remained in 'a prohibited zone' for centuries. That's why, the female dramatic tradition in India is not as formidable as the male dramatic tradition. Actually, the feminist theatre world over is:

> ...politically aligned to the ideas of the post-1968 women's movement and is concerned with ways in which woman's perceptions have been resolved by the particular nature of the female body. It is interested in seeking new ways

> of making knowledge from the viewpoint of the body. (Kapur: 5)

Though the state of feminist theatre through female tradition in India is considerably subsidiary, it should be accepted that it is responsible for adding significant subjects such as sexual division of labour, mothering, prescriptive roles and gender stereotypes, female friendship, female sexuality and the political importance of identity to the dramatic canon in India. In this way, it paves a way to study the multiple aspects related to a woman's life. It has become a powerful medium to tackle the different issues determining woman's socio-political position.

Bharati Sarabhai the only recognized woman playwright before Independence staged her dramatic excellence through her plays, viz. *The Well of the People* and *Two Women*. The significance of Sarabhai is her experimental attitude. She wrote these plays in two different forms. Actually, it was a difficult task for women writers before Independence to attempt drama for literary expression. But Bharati Sarabhai accepted the challenge and ventured to stage her dramatic merit. But the women playwrights after her could not accelerate the standard of presentation to great extent. They could not extensively contribute or there was rarely an experimental concern in their performances. It was necessary to encourage women writers to opt drama as their major creative faculty. But it was altogether a difficult task. The socio-cultural structure before Independence and after some decades of Independence did not allow easily woman's participation in public affairs. Actually, drama is not complete without performance. But it was certainly difficult for these one or two women playwrights to take their plays for performance in a theatre house. The women playwrights such as K.B. Thakur, J.B. Billomoria, Swarnakumari Devi Ghosal, Arti Nagarwala, Kamala Subramaian modeled their plays either on classical model or contributed marginally to sustain the female tradition. They preferred certainly the issues of women for their dramatic presentation. But could not voice their expression, substantially. They failed to represent most of the issues directly or indirectly related to woman's being. Indian woman's domestic and public life was either restricted or completely unexplored.

The generally accepted consideration was that a stream cannot rise above its source. It was not really expected that women should indulge themselves in writing and performing the plays. The lack of encouragement certainly caused a setback as far the development of female tradition in Indian English Drama concerned.

The mid-twentieth century could see some favourable changes as far the participation of women writers in dramatic growth in India is in view. The talented playwrights such as Dina Mehta, Poile Sengupta and Manjula Padmanabhan are among the leaders of women playwriting of this phase. There is a novelty in their dramatic expression. They are responsible to introduce a wide range of subjects to Indian English Drama. There is not any biased or prejudiced expression in them. The expression is more pragmatic and realistic. There is a perfect balance in their expression. The plays of Dina Mehta illustrate the social status of Indian woman whereas the plays of Poile Sengupta document the varied aspects of woman's life. There is a scholarly attribution of woman's actual living in these plays. On the other hand, Manjula Padmanabhan illustrates a new image of Indian woman through her plays. In this way, there is a different and more realistic position of Indian woman in the plays of these playwrights.

The contemporary women playwrights have substantially contributed to strengthen the female tradition of drama in India. The changed socio-cultural set up might have caused a remarkable growth in this regard. The women writers in India are capable enough to single out the field of their interest. Hence, there is both standard and variety in their literary expression. The basic difference between the earlier women playwrights and the late twentieth century women dramatists is the way they refuse the male created experience to construct the experience based on their own imagination. It is certainly an innovative initiative they have undertaken to build up a better future. Yet, it is necessary to have more women playwrights making the actual picture more effective. Actually, drama is instrumental to tackle the issues related to woman's life. Women can make their expression more impressive with the help of drama.

The male dramatic tradition of pre-Independence phase witnessed dramaturgy of dramatists such as Sri Aurobindo, Rabindranath Tagore, Pratap Sharma and Harishchandra Chattopadhyay. These playwrights, in a real sense, shaped the Indian English Drama of this phase. S.K. Bhatta (1987: 9) argues: "This phase presents plays and playlets, the themes of which are from legends and epics, events from history and the problems of contemporary society." The contemporary social problems were at the centre of these plays. But these problems were mainly confronted by the male members of the society. The socio-cultural scenario in their plays was restricted particularly to the hurdles in the day-to-day living of men. Mostly the epic characters were considered as an inspiration as the life was modeled on the epic ideals. The dichotomy between men and women was a contrasting presentation of their image through drama. As it is in other literary genres, there is a realistic presentation of social issues in drama. The predominant male dramatic tradition illustrated the fact that woman is restricted to home. She is either worshiped or cursed. There was a rare consideration of her struggle for day-to-day survival. Her subordination in power structure was not highlighted to support her but to signify, overall state of woman in our conventional society. Emphasizing her position, it can be further argued that

> ...progressively tied her down to the home and withdrew her from the economic, political and religious areas of social participation. Paralleling these two processes, these took place the progressive elaboration of an ideology which rationalized this shift from differention to discrimination and institutionalized it by means of custom, rituals and religious or social prescriptions. (Mukherjee: 40)

The prejudiced deliberations regarding woman's social stature was central to the most of the plays in male-dramatic tradition of this phase.

The post-Independence Indian English Drama grew steadily both in quality and quantity. It enjoyed the status of being a comprehensive delineation of Indian social life. Being a prominent drama figure of this phase, Asif Currimbhoy spearheaded the canon with a concern for social issues and most particularly to the newly emerged conflict between old and new ideas. At the same time, his plays were structured on Elizabethan model. On the other hand, Pratap Sharma, one more prominent playwright of the phase, presented the theme of sex in a different way. His dramatic proficiency took the subject of his plays to a crest. Besides Asif Currimbhoy, Nissim Ezekiel has a prestige of being an illustrious dramatic figure. But on the other hand, the drama of these leading playwrights substantially failed to present the world of women through their plays. The corpus could not explore completely woman's self as it gave a little importance to her issues. There is not an elaboration of woman's life in these plays. Her pathetic condition under patriarchy was not really stated in their plays. There was a little scope to realize the actual state of Indian women in their plays.

The makers of 'The New Drama' in India Vijay Tendulkar, Badal Sircar, Girish Karnad and Mohan Rakesh elaborated the difficult world of modern individuals through their plays. But their treatment differs widely from each other. In the plays of Mohan Rakesh, the issues of modern life have been tackled with a prior consideration of day-to-day situation. Vijay Tendulkar binds socio-political reality in his plays. There is a harsh satire on the power system of his time in his plays. On the other hand, Girish Karnad intrigues myth with contemporary life to unearth the socio-political condition. Badal Sircar through his 'Third Theatre' undermines the theatre and rural Indian society. But to a great extent, there remains an incomplete perception of women's world in the plays of these prominent playwrights. On the other hand, the plays of Bharati Sarabhai, Mahasweta Devi and Manjula Padmanabhan, the leading women playwrights, discover the world of women through an illustration of gender-centred reality.

II

The gender-based social reality unearths the different aspects constituting woman's image in our conventional society. It foregrounds the causes behind a stereotyped construction of woman's image in male-dominated society. The fundamental principles of Marxist-Feminist theory substantially help to establish a link between woman's social existence and biased construction of her sex. Further, it helps to deconstruct the patriarchal erection of a woman to constitute a differing image of woman, standing firmly on the basis of subjectivity. To state further, "Woman had", Irigary conceded, "been defined as the figure through which man comes to know, master and differentiate himself, but one could also imagine another mode of subjectivity. Such a mode would be sexually different and autonomous. Woman would not be man's other" (Plain and Sellers: 221). In this way, the gender-centred interpretation is an attempt to differentiate woman from man with a strong consideration of her individuality. The women playwrights such as Bharati Sarabhai, Mahasweta Devi and Manjula Padmanabhan have, to some extent, elaborated woman's social stature to show how woman has been subordinated in patriarchal society. On the other hand, the protagonists of their plays strife to liberate themselves and attend the long-awaited 'wilde zone' in their life.

Old woman's longing in *The Well of the People* to visit shrines such as Kashi and Haridwar, at least once in her life, illustrates the conventional spirituality preparing a woman's mind to the extent of considering pilgrimage as vocation. She has been insisted to visit the shrines after demise of her son and husband for salvation of their souls. But the advent of Gandhian socio-spiritualism transforms her faith, completely. Now she decides to build a well for the untouchables of her village out of the money she saved for her dream pilgrimage. A woman has been constructed in our society in such a way that she fails to develop her individual standpoint. But here she is assisted to attend subjectivity with an emerging ideology. Bharati Sarabhai emphasizes a woman's successful venture in male-dominated society to meet the other side of her personality. At the same time, Bharati Sarabhai dramatizes the agony of peasants and workers under the cruelty of Britishers and usurers.

The assorted aspect of Indian womanhood is the subject of her other play *Two Women*. The playwright explores the facet of Indian womanhood, constructed under patriarchy. How a woman's significance in the inner and outer world is considerably neglected in our phallocentric society is subject of the play. The male dominance makes it extremely difficult for a woman to have any social significance to her life. But the other aspect is disclosed through Urvashi Devi's insurgent thinking. She accepts an anti-patriarchal position in her life because she is alienated from the present male-dominated world. To the end, she helps her friend to challenge the conventional restrictions for a woman to take decision of her choice. In this way, one woman helps another to resolve individuality. She helps her to know the other world conveying a different reality. Bharati Sarabhai accentuates the essence of woman's individual stand in male-dominated society in both of her plays.

Mahasweta Devi in her plays perceives the gender-centred social reality by challenging the notions of conventional motherhood. She ensures a strong, solid and firm stand to Sujata Chatterjee and Chandidasi in *Mother of 1084* and *Bayen* respectively through the impressive actions performed by them. Sujata Chatterjee undergoes an odyssey to unearth the reasons behind her Naxalite son Brati's death. She challenges her own restricted bourgeois image by revealing the outside reality before the so-called gentlemen and women. It is mother in a woman that provides enough tenacity to disarm the phallocentric restrictions. Sujata's journey simultaneously denotes Mahasweta Devi's endeavour to apprehend the inclination of young generation of her time towards Naxalite movement. The playwright, in this way, denotes the reality related to the life in Kolkata of late seventies before her readers. On the other hand, she illustrates a mother's journey from vocation to apotheosis in the play *Bayen*. A woman denotes herself for a social cause. She sacrifices her motherhood for the cause of community. But the patriarchal society fails to acknowledge her endurance for a noble cause. Instead of rewarding her for sincere efforts, she is being tormented and defamed as a witch. The social pressure consequences into dishonour of a woman. There lies a tangible difference between a woman's honesty and dishonesty in male-dominated society. Chandi's efforts are easily disregarded and she is punished on the charge of Necromancy. But her son Bhagirath defies the patriarchal decoding and reconstruct subjectivity of her mother.

Mahasweta Devi enlarges subsistence of women to form their social significance. In this way, she illustrates woman's power through Sujata and Chandi after an open challenge to their motherhood.

Manjula Padmanabhan, a leading contemporary playwright, emphasizes contemporary social reality in her plays *Lights Out* and *Harvest*. Both the plays accentuate the changed social pattern in the contemporary world. The play *Lights Out* explores the middle-class urban hypocrisy. A group of men and women continue to discuss the issue of a woman's molestation taking place before their eyes. The playwright considers this meaningless discussion as a severe form of violence. No one among them comes down to save the woman from the brutal. Manjula Padmanabhan condemns this tendency of the so-called sophisticated individuals who fail to do anything meaningful to free the woman from the goondas. The play ends on the note of inertia of middle-class individuals resulting in a woman's deformity. The playwright strikes at the tendency of the so-called sophisticated individuals who harm the social integrity through their inactive engagements. The play emphasizes at the same time, escapism of the urban people. On the other hand, the play *Harvest* explores the commodification of human bodies in the postmodern world. It focuses on it as an aspect of postmodern social reality. The growing impact of occult economy on the lives of Third World men and women has been harming their life to the worst. The playwright treats the conflict between the First and the Third World as a consequence of growing capitalism. Om, a chawl resident sells his organs for material gadgets. He is being compelled to do it by his family members. Except his wife Jaya, no one else in the family opposes his plan to sell the organs. But the other members of the family consider it as an opportunity to gain all the pleasures they have desired in their life. But the end of all this is extremely painful. They loss whatever they have gained due to their unstoppable greed. Altogether, Manjula Padmanabhan unearths the real contemporary urban life in both of her plays.

The playwrights such as Bharati Sarabhai, Mahasweta Devi and Manjula Padmanabhan elaborate the gender-centred reality in their respective plays. They connote the dominant aspects of social realism constituting a woman's position in the male-dominated society.

III

The psychodynamics of language intends to discover the journey of woman protagonists to meet the world of their experience through an expression of liberation. The expression of these liberated individuals helps to form their self to attend subjectivity ultimately. In other words, it becomes a voyage to gain their liberated self. Julia Kristeva's coinage Semiotic is significant to identify the ability of women characters for securing the language for self-expression. The socio-cultural patriarchal dominance has suppressed their utmost efforts to liberate but their continuous struggle is really appreciable.

The psycho-feminist criticism of Helen Cixous, Julia Kristeva and Nancy Chodorow is poignant to explore the different aspects of this psychological journey which has a fruitful ending in form of woman's own language.

Old woman in Bharati Sarabhai's *The Well of the People* hesitates initially to go straight with the language of self-expression. She finds it extremely difficult to interact in a male-dominated world. But the advent of Gandhism helps her to release from this difficulty and convey the decision of her will. Her endeavour to meet subjectivity strengthens her expression. It gives her enough capability to go against conventional ideology and communicate discourse of liberation. The other play *Two Women* interacts the difference of expression in two women characters in the play. Urvashi Devi is able to communicate, to use Kristeva'a term, Semiotic. On the other hand, Anuradha is in difficulty to release herself from the conventional impressions on her mind. But Urvashi helps her for the possible and expected transformation. It gives her enough strength to interact in her self-centred discourse. The playwright, all the way, accentuates the world of woman's experience through their aspiration to constitute a liberated self. Bharati Sarabhai illustrates the difficulty of women in obtaining the language of self-expression in a phallocentric society. But they aspire to meet their subjectivity by realizing significance of self-discourse, to the end.

Mahasweta Devi demonstrates the problem of women in male-dominated society to cultivate their personal expression. Sujata Chattejee in *Mother of 1084* is a typical bourgeois woman who has lost her ability to communicate in own language. She is unable initially to challenge the unnatural behaviour of her husband and the other family members after the death of her son Brati. But after meeting with Nandini and Somu's mother, she shows enough strength to convey her discomfort with their stand. In this way, she unearths her individuality, to the end of the play. On the other hand, *Bayen* emphasizes a low-caste woman's plight through her unending dissociation from the lords of her society. Chandidasi strives her level best to take care of the responsibilities shouldered on her after the death of her father. But the society disregards sacrifice and consideration as it ostracizes her on the charge of Necromancy. But before that she dares to convey her denial to dig and keep the graves to her community. Mahasweta Devi illustrates the power of woman's liberated expression in both of her plays.

Manjula Padmanabhan distinguishes her dramatic expression through her plays *Lights Out* and *Harvest*. The play *Lights Out* being a discussion play unearths hypocritical discourse of middle-class individuals. The woman characters such as Naina and Leela emphasize their biased language under phallocentric subsumption. On the other hand, silence of Frieda is the language of suppression of a woman in patriarchy. She has lost her ability to speak in the men-dominated world. It is quite difficult for her to express herself. In this way, the playwright shows both the aspects of woman's language in the play. The play *Harvest* presents a woman's difficulty through Jaya's character to accept a particular language in phallocentric system. Manjula Padmanabhan gives a radical expression to the woman's language in both of her plays.

On the other hand, the dramaturgy of Bharati Sarabhai, Mahasweta Devi and Manjula Padmanabhan differentiate them from the other playwrights on the basis of implementation of innovative stage devices. The stage strategy captivates readers' attention due to newness in presentation. It gives them opportunity to demonstrate their plays in an effective way to accentuate woman's status in our society.

IV

Bharati Sarabhai incorporates different forms for the presentation of her plays: *The Well of the People* and *Two Women*. Her play *The Well of the People* is a versical attempt. The play is based on certain verse compositions. It is a prototype of Sarabhai's captivation for a poetic expression. The beautiful use of poetry makes the expression more effective. The play renders considerably from Yeatsian model of Poetic Drama and also Eliot's poetic experiments in *Murder in the Cathedral*. The playwright elaborates old woman's transformation in an effective way with the help of appropriate verse. In her other play *Two Women* the major focus is on to present two different world of Anuradha and Urvashi, the old mates. The entire play takes place in Kanak Raya's sitting room. The use of stage devices is remarkable due to a balanced presentation. The playwright divides the sitting room in two parts to show the different ideological stands. Kanak is Western in his appearance whereas his wife Anuradha is a conventional, religious woman. The playwright depicts here an internal conflict through division of sitting room in two parts. Bharati Sarabhai names Anuradha's part as 'Radha's Corner' to illustrate her inclination for Krishna Bhakti. The personification of Himalaya is also significant in the play. It is an example of Bharati Sarabhai's crafty stage handling. The use of lights is also crucial in the play. Bharati Sarabhai implements versical form in *The Well of the People* whereas *Two Women* is a prose type. But the stage strategy is highly appreciable in both of these plays.

Mahasweta Devi has an intimacy with Augusto Boal's Theatre of the Oppressed in both of her plays as far stage strategy is concerned. Her play *Mother of 1084* enacts a single day in the life of protagonist of the play Sujata Chatterjee. As there is a considerable importance to the gestures in the plays of Augusto Boal, similarly Mahasweta Devi shows a concern for gestures of her protagonist. Sujata's gestures demonstrate a significant meaning in the play. Besides, the use of tape-recorder as a stage device proves Mahasweta Devi's simple handling. Basically, Mahasweta Devi's theatre is for under-privileged, marginalized people. Therefore, she maintains an utmost simplicity in her presentation. On the other hand, she uses the gestures in *Bayen* to emphasize the different aspects. Malinder moves from the present to the past with the help of meaningful gestures. The gestures become the mode of his expression. Mahasweta Devi maintains theatrical economy and denotes a deep level meaning in both the plays.

Manjula Padmanabhan being a leading contemporary playwright demonstrates a crafty use of Brechtian gestures in her play *Lights Out*. She illustrates typical middle-class hypocrisy through the use of meaningful gestures. The play *Harvest* is an example of effective use of modern technological devices. The use of contact modular is significant in the play. The playwright uses some other technological instruments in the play to link her presentation with the modern lifestyle. Manjula Padmanabhan's technicality helps to present a wide angel of experiences related to woman's individuality.

The focus of the work in the preceding chapters is centred to explore gender centered reality, semiotic and stage devices in the selected plays to elaborate the world of woman's experience. It also aims at differentiating these plays from the dominant dramatic culture in India. Further, it illustrates the place of these playwrights and also the findings.

V

The contribution of Bharati Sarabhai, Mahasweta Devi and Manjula Padmanabhan can be measured through their successful ventures in exploring new womanhood through the trials of their women protagonists in the plays. The new womanhood arises here out of the efforts of women protagonists to free their souls to experience 'a wild zone'. The women protagonists with a different socio-cultural background dare to defy the dominant patriarchal system. The protagonists of Bharati Sarabhai are not absolutely individual but they have enough potential to demolish patriarchal ideology restraining their personal existence.

Old woman of *The Well of the People* dares to challenge the stereotyped construction of Indian woman in our conventional society by taking decision of her choice. The socio-cultural image of Indian woman is now replaced with a new image to provide enough endurance to have a choice of decision-making. Actually, it is a psychological transformation that helps her to come out of 'a mute agreement'. On the other hand, Bharati Sarabhai denotes the contrasting aspects of Indian womanhood in her play *Two Women*. She shows here how a woman is capable to speak the language of liberation after realizing self. At the same time, the realization helps the other woman to come out from the androcentric perceptions of life.

Bharati Sarabhai's dramaturgy is significant for its sturdy literary expression. When the other women writers in India were interested in poetry or fiction, Sarabhai used drama as a medium of her literary expression. In the midst of unfavourable atmosphere, Bharati Sarabhai strived to depict the genuine position of Indian woman through her plays. She might have realized that drama is the most appropriate literary form to tackle the issues related to woman's self and subjectivity. In this way, her dramatic contribution initiates a new phase for women's writing in India.

On the other hand, Mahasweta Devi, an activist-writer, documents the realities of life through her writing. Motherhood provides enough strength to her protagonists. Sujata Chatterjee and Chandidasi withstand the conventional patriarchal ideology with the help of mother's sensibility. Mother in them strives to resist in the midst of social despondency. Mahasweta Devi explores another aspect of womanhood which is close to the conception of reliance and affection for the mother on the earth. It is through mother's image they are aspired to depict their innocence.

Manjula Padmanabhan, a niche among the contemporary Indian English playwrights, demonstrates the factual state of Indian women in her plays. She defers to some extent from Bharati Sarabhai and Mahasweta Devi while illustrating woman of her time in her plays. She aspires to enlarge image of a new woman in her plays. But at the same time, she does not excuse them for their personal idiocy. She is sympathetic towards Frieda, one of the victims in her play *Lights Out*. But at the same time, she hammers the hypocritic tendency of Leela and Naina. On the other hand, she is humanistic towards Jaya but does not take easily vicious nature of Ma in her award winning play *Harvest*. In this way, she discloses both the aspects of Indian womanhood.

These *avant-garde* women playwrights have helped to substantiate the scope for involvement of more women writers in the field of drama. The use of innovative stage devices in their plays is also one of the dominant aspects of difference and merit as far the position of these playwrights is concerned. These playwrights have provided possible resilience for the growth of woman's drama in our country. They have demonstrated something significant through content, language and techniques in their plays. On the other hand, the quintessence of the plays discussed here is the presence of feminine consciousness in them. The playwrights accentuate the consciousness of their characters through the subject of their plays, the language these characters adopt in course of time and the stage devices implemented to sustain personal consciousness. These playwrights look at woman's world as 'a fertile land of experience'. They show an immense interest in exploring an authentic experience of their women characters. They prefer to release the women characters from the boundaries of class and caste so that suppression under patriarchy can be replaced with self-liberation. The concern for self and subjectivity is absolutely pivotal in these plays. Altogether, Bharati Sarabhai, Mahasweta Devi and Manjula Padmanabhan have succeeded in doing justice with female identity. Thus, their contribution needs to be considered as a predominant one for the growth of women's playwriting in India. On the other hand, the dramatic contribution of Bharati Sarabhai, Mahasweta Devi and Manjula Padmanabhan is pivotal in the formation of a new society because it has certain significant features related to the formation a new society based on equal consideration of woman's social stature, language and her importance in decision-making. At the same time, the plays contribute to demolish the stereotyped, conventionally constructed social image of a woman and give a fresh, balanced interpretation of her image and exercise a vital role in the formation of a new society.

VI

The book states the findings such as presence of female consciousness in the selected plays, representation of Indian womanhood, an initiative to explore woman's world of experience, an urge to develop woman's language to release her from phallocentric subsumption, a comprehensive outlook of woman's psyche or psychological transformation, a serious consideration of gender-centred reality and significance of these plays in sustaining 'female voice' in Indian theatre. On the other hand, it emphasizes the need to substantiate contribution and certain defects in the plays of these playwrights. At certain places, these plays fail to match with the plays in dominant tradition. But the attribution of these plays is definitely noticeable. They occupy a respective position in the galaxy of women's drama in India.

The present book is crucial to open certain research avenues in the field of women's theatre to accelerate the velocity of research in Indian women's drama. It certainly encourages exploring the neglected world of women in our literary canon. It emphasizes the fact that drama can be effective and instrumental to tackle the real world of women. The women writers can enact the diverse aspects of Indian womanhood by demonstrating their real world. It enlarges the canvas of women's experience and shows the woman's dramatic tradition equally significant to the dominant male tradition in Indian English Drama. It insists the fact that the corpus is a ray of hope to ensconce an unprejudiced perception of Indian woman's world of experience and also to explore womanhood by offering a perspicacious criticism on Indian woman's personal as well as social life. At the same time, it conveys the assurance of these plays to develop the female tradition in Indian English Drama equally vibrant to the Western female dramatic tradition and be central to the dominant dramatic culture like it. The gender-centric study of the women protagonists in the plays here accentuates the need to reshape the very presence of women in society in general and literary works in particular. But it is possible after challenging the model produced, developed, and owned by male writers. There is need to re-explore the issues of women and treat them by putting their concern at the central position. The implementation is next to impossible without women writers' realization first and association next to create a world of women's experience. It is more appropriate and necessary in terms of drama because drama is close to woman's life. It has been the most suitable medium to elaborate her concerns and feelings unfortunately left undiscovered in male dominated society. But there is a need to take collective efforts to create an electrifying effect. Then only Indian women's theatre would be at the centre of the dramatic culture in India.

References

Bhatta, S.K. (1987). *Indian Drama in English: A Critical Study.* New Delhi. Sterling Publication.

Dharwadkar, Aparna (2005). *Theatres of Independence.* New Delhi: Oxford University Press.

Kapur, Anuradha (2001). "A Wandering Word: An Unstable Subject." *Theatre India.* National School of Drama. 2:3 (May): 5-12.

Mukherjee, Parth, N. "Sex and Social Structure." cited in Vikas Rawal's *Women Characters in Post-Independence Indian English Drama.* Jaipur: Vital Publications, 16-25.

Plain, Gill and Sellers, Susan (2005). *A History of Feminist Literary Criticism.* Cambridge: Cambridge University Press.

Simion, Shepherd and Wallis, Mick (2004). *Drama/Theatre/ Performance.* New York: Routledge.

Bibliography

Secondary Sources: Books and Dissertations

Althuser, Louis (1977). *For Marx*. London: Verso.

Alyosius, G. (1997). *Nationalism Without a Nation in India*. New Delhi: Oxford University Press.

Asthana, Pratima (1974). *Woman's Movement in India*. Delhi: Vikas.

Austin, J.L. (1976). *How to Do Things with Words*. Oxford: Oxford University Press.

Banks, O. (1981). *Faces of Feminism*. Oxford: Martin Robertson.

Barba, Euginio and Savarese, Nicola (1991). *The Secret Art of the Performer*. London: Routledge.

Barret, Michele (1981). *Women's Oppression Today: Problems in Marxist Feminist Analysis*. New York: Schocken Books.

Barret, M. and Phillips, A. (1992). Editors. *Destabilizing Theory: Contemporary Feminist Debates*. Cambridge: Polity Press.

Beasley, Chris (1999). *Feminism*. London: Sage Publications Limited.

Bebel, A. (1971). *Women Under Socialism*. New York: Schocken Books.

Benegal, Som (1967). *A Panorama of Theatre in India*. New Delhi: Indian Council for Cultural Relations.

Bhushan, V.N. (1945). *The Blazing Shine: Anthology of One-Act Plays in English by Women Writers*. Bombay: Padma Publications.

Bharagava, Raju (Ed.) (2002). *Indian Writing in English: The Last Decade*. New Delhi: Rawat Publications.

Bhatia, Nandi (2004). *Acts of Authority/Acts of Resistance: Theatre and Politics in Colonial and Post-Colonial India*. New Delhi: Oxford University Press.

Bhatta, S.K. (1987). *Indian English Drama: A Critical Study*. New Delhi: Sterling Publications Pvt. Ltd.

Bial, Henry (Ed.) (2007). *The Performance Studies Reader*. New York: Routledge.

Blanchot Maurice (1982). *The Space of Literature*. Trans. Ann Smock. Lincoln: University of Nebraska Press.

Blum, Harold (1977). *Female Psychology: Contemporary Psychoanalytic Views*. New York: International University Press.

Bock, G. and Thane, P. (Eds.) (1991). *Maternity and Gender Policies*. London: Routledge.

Braidotti, Rosi (1990). *Patterns of Dissonance: A Study of Women in Contermporary Philosophy*. Cambridge. Polity Press.

Brater, Enoch (Ed.) (1989). *Feminine Focus: The New Women Playwrights*. New York and Oxford: Oxford University Press.

Brown, Janet (1979). *Feminist Drama: Definition and Critical Analysis*. London: Scarecrow Press.

Brooks, Cleanth *et al.* (1972). *Understanding Drama*. London: Penguin.

Brook, Peter (1990). *The Empty Space*. London: Penguin.

Brecht, Brtolt (1964). *Brecht on Theatre: The Development of Aesthetic*. Editor and Trans. John Willet. New York: Hill and Wang.

Butler, Judith (1990). *Gender Trouble: Feminism and the Subversion* of *Identity*. New York: Routledge.

_____ (1997). *Excitable Speech: A Politics of the Performance*. New York and London: Routledge.

Byrski, M. Cristopher (1974). *Concept of Ancient Indian Theatre*. New Delhi: Munshiram Manoharlal Publishers Pvt. Ltd.

Campbell, A.A. (2002). *Mind of One's Own: The Evolutionary Psychology of Women*. New York: Oxford University Press.

Campbell, Petrick (Ed.) (1986). *Analyzing Performance*. Manchester: Manchester University Press.

Case, sue Ellen (Ed.) (1988). *Performing Feminisms: Critical Theory and Theatre*. New York: Methuen.

Chodorow, Nancy (1978). *Reproducuction of Mothering: Psychoanalysis and Sociology of Gender*. Berkeley: University of California Press.

Chakrabarty, Bandana and Talwar, Urmila (Eds.) (2005). *Contemporary Indian Drama: Astride Two Traditions*. New Delhi: Rawat Publications.

Chakravarthy, Radha (2008). *Feminism and Contemporary Women Writers: Redefining Subjectivity*. New Delhi: Routledge.

Chatterjee, P. (1989). *The Nation and its Fragments: Colonial and Postcolonial Histories*. Bombay: Oxford University Press.

Chaudhari, Maitrayee (1993). *Indian Women's Movement: Reform and Revival*. New Delhi: Radiant.

Chenge, Anne Anlin (2001). *The Melancholy of Race: Psychoanalysis, Assimilation, and Hidden Grief*. Oxford: Oxford University Press.

Cornell, Drucilla (1991). *Beyond Accommodation: Ethical Feminism, Deconstruction and the Law*. New York: Routledge.

Dalmia, Vasudha (2006). *Poetics, Plays and Performances: The Politics of Modern Indian Theatre*. New Delhi: Oxford University Press.

Dass, Veena Noble (1995). *Critical Events: An Anthropological Perspective on Contemporary India*. Delhi: Oxford University Press.

____ (1998). *Modern Indian Drama in English Translation*. Hyderabad: Taurus.

Daly, Mary (1985). *Beyond God the Father: Towards a Philosophy of Women's Liberation*. London: The Women's Press.

Dally, Ann (1982). *Inventing Motherhood: The Consequence of an Ideal*. London: Burnett.

David, Donald (2001). *Subjective, Intersubjective Objective*. Oxford: Oxford University Press.

Davis, Angtela, Y. (1981). *Women, Race and Class*. New York: Random House.

Davidson, Donald (2005). *Truth, Language and History*. Oxford: Oxford University Press.

Dean, Tim (2000). *Beyond Sexuality*. Chicago: University of Chicago Press.

Deshpande, G.P. (Ed.) (2000). *Modern Indian Drama: An Anthology*. New Delhi: Sahitya Akademi.

Deutsch, Helene (1973). *The Psychology of Women*. II. New York: Bantam.

Devi, Mahasweta (1997). *Five Plays*. Trans. Samik Bandyopadhyay. Calcutta: Seagull Books.

Devy, G.N. (1992). *After Amnesia: Tradition and Change in Indian Literary Criticism*. Bombay: Orient Longman.

Dharwadkar, Aparna (2005). *Theatres of Independence*. New Delhi: Oxford University Press.

Dinah, Luise Leavitt (1980). *Feminist Theatre Groups* McFarland: Jefferson NC.

Dolan, Jill (1998). *The Feminist Spectator as Critic*. Ann Arbor: UMI Reserver Press.

Donovan, Josephine (1975). *Feminist Literary Criticism: Explorations in Theory*. Lexington: University of Kentucky Press.

Eakin, B.W. and R.G. Eakins (1978). *Sex Difference in Human Communication*. Boston: Houghton Mufflin.

Edward, Thompson (1926). *Rabindrnath: Poet and Dramatist.* London: Oxford University Press.

Eisenstein, H. (1984). *Contemporary Feminist Thought.* London: George Allen & Unwin.

Eisenstein, Z. (1984). *Feminism and Sexual Equality.* New York: Monthly Review Press.

Elam, Keir (1991). *Semiotics of Theatre and Drama.* London: Routledge.

Ellmann, Mary (1978). *Thinking about Women.* Harcourt: Brace & World.

Elshtain, J.B. (1981). *Public Man, Private Woman: Women in Social and Political Thought.* Princeton: Princeton University Press.

Evans, J. (1995). *Feminist Theory Today.* London: Sage.

Everrett, Jane Matson (1979). *Woman and Social Change in India.* New Delhi: Heritage.

Fausto-Sterling, A. (1993). *Myths of Gender: Biological Theories about Women and Men.* New York: Basic Books.

Figes, Eva (1987). *Patriarchal Attitudes: Women in Society.* New York: Persea Books.

Frost, Anthony and Yarrow, Ralph (1990). *Improvisation in Drama.* London: Macmillan.

Foley, D. (1986). *Understanding Capital.* Cambridge: Harvard University Press.

Gandhi, Nandita and Shah, Namita (2007). *The Issues at Stake: Theory and Practice in the Contemporary Women's Movement in India.* New Delhi: Kali for Women & The Book Review Literary Trust.

Gargi, Balwant (1962). *Theatre in India.* New York: Theatre Art Books.

____ (1966). *Folk Theatre of India.* Seatle: University of Washington Press.

Gallop, Jane (1982). *Feminism and Psychoanalysis: The Daughter's Seduction.* London: Macmillan.

Geetha, V. (2000). Gender. Calcutta: Stree.

Gilligan, Carol (1980). *In a Different Voice: Psychological Theory and Women's Development*. Chicago and London: Harvard University Press.

Goldstein, Laurence (Ed.) (1994). *The Male Body: Features, Destinies, Exposures*. Ann Arbor: Michigan University Press.

Goodman, Lynda and Jane de Gay (Eds.) (1999). *The Routledge Reader in Gender and Performance*. New York: Routledge.

Goodman, Lizabeth (1993). *Contemporary Feminist Theatres: To Each of Her Own*. London and New York: Routledge.

Gorant, J. (1993). *Fundamental Feminism*. New York: Routledge.

Greene, Gayle and Kahn Coppelia (Ed.) (1985). *Making Difference: Feminist Literary Criticism*. New York and London: Routledge.

Griffin, Susan. (1978). *Woman and Nature: The Roaring Inside Her*. New York: Harper and Row.

Gruber, Ruth (2005). *Virginia Woolf: The Will to Create as a Woman*. New York: Carroll & Graf.

Gupt, Bharat (1989). *Dramatic Concepts: Greek and Indian*. New Delhi: D.K. Print World Pvt. Ltd.

Harish, Ranjana and Harishankar, B.V. (Eds.) (2008). *Re-defining Feminism*. New Delhi: Rawat Publications.

Harn Holtby, Winifred (1934). *Women and a Changing Civilization*. London: John Lane.

Hart, Lynda (Ed.) (1989). *Making a Spectacle: Feminist Essays on Contemporary Women's Theatre*. Michigan: University of Michigan Press.

Haraia-White, Barbara (2003). *India Working: Essays on Society and Economy*. Cambridge: Cambridge University Press.

Hasan, Ardent (1970). *On Violence*. New York: Bruce and World Inc.

Heidegger, Martin (1962). *Being and Time*. Trans. J. Macquarie and E. Robinson. Oxford: Blackwell.

Heilbrun, Carolyn (1974). *Toward a Recognition of Androgyny.* New York: Harper Colophon Books.

Hickey, L. (Ed.) (1990). *The Pragmatics of Style.* London: Routledge.

Iyengar, Srinivas K.R. (1973). *Indian Writing in English.* Bombay: Sterling Publication Limited.

Jackson, S. and Jones, J. (Ed.) (1998). *Contemporary Feminist Theatres.* New York: University Press.

Jain, Jasbir (1996). *Women's Writing: Text and Context.* Jaipur: Rawat Publications.

Jane, Gallop (1982). *The Daughter's Seduction: Feminism and Psychoanalysis.* New York: Ithaca.

Janet, Brown (1979). *Feminist Drama: Definition and Critical Analysis.* London: Scarecrow Press.

Jayawardena, K. (Ed.) (1986). *Feminism and Nationalism in the Third World.* London: Zed Press.

Jeffreyes, S. (1990). *Anti-Climax: A Feminist Perspective of the Sexual Revolution.* London: Women's Press.

Jung, Anees (1987). *Unveiling India: A Woman's Journay.* New Delhi: Penguin Books.

Kar, Prafulla C. (Ed.) (1997). *Critical Theory: Western and Indian.* New Delhi. Pencraft International.

Kaur, Amrit (1946). *Challenge to Women.* Allahabad: New Literature.

Keysser, Helene (1984). *Feminist Theatre.* London: Macmillan.

____ (1996). *Feminist Theatre and Theory.* London: Macmillan.

Kishwar, Madhu (1986). *Gandhi and Women.* Delhi: Manushi Prakashan.

Kristeva, Julia (1984). *Revolution in Poetic Language.* Trans. Margaret Waller. New York: Columbia University Press.

____. (1991). *Strangers to Ourselves.* Trans. Leon S. Roudiez. New York: Columbia University Press.

Kumar, R. (1993). *History of Doing.* New Delhi: Kali for Women.

Lakoff, Robin (1975). *Language and Woman's Place*. New York: P. Harper Road.

Liddle, Joanna and Joshi, Rama (1986). *Daughter of Independence: Gender Caste and Class in India*. London: Zed Books.

Londes, J.P. (Ed.) (1998). *Feminism: The Public and the Private*. Oxford: Oxford University Press.

Machwe, Prabhakar (1979). *Modernity and Contemporary Indian Theatre*. New Delhi: Chetna.

Macoby, Eleanor and Jacklin Carol (1974). *The Psychology of Sex Difference*. Stanford: Stanford University Press.

Mahler, Margaret S. (1979). *Separation Individuation*. New York: Aronson P.

Malekin, Peter and Yarrow, Ralph (1997). *Consciousness, Literature and Theory: Theory and Beyond*. London: Macmillan.

Marx, Karl (1973). *The German Ideology*. New York: International Publishers.

McDowell, John (1996). *Mind and World*. Cambridge M.A.: Harvard University Press.

Mee, B. Erin (Ed.) (2001). *Drama Contemporary India*. Oxford: Oxford University Press.

Menon, Nivedita (1999). *Gender and Politics in India*. New Delhi: Oxford University Press.

Mehta, Dina (1993). *Brides are not for Burning*. New Delhi: Rupa & Co.

Mestrovic, Stipan G. (1997). *Postcolonial Society*. London: Sage Publications.

Miller, Jean Braker (1976). *Toward a New Psychology of Women*. Boston: Beacon Press.

Millr, Nancy K. (Ed.) (1986). *The Poetics of Gender*. New York: Columbia University Press.

_____ (1988). *Subject to Change: Reading Feminist Writing*. New York: Columbia University Press.

Mitchell, J. (1975). *Psychoanalysis and Feminism.* Penguin: London.

Mitchll, Juliette and Jacqueline Rose (1984). *Feminine Sexuality: Jacques Lacan and the ecole freudienne.* New York: W.W. Norton.

Mitchell, J. and Oakely, A. (1986). *What is Feminine*? Blackwell: Oxford.

Mitter, S. (1986). *Common Fate, Common Bond: Women in the Global Economy*. London: Pluto.

Moghdam, Valentine, M. (Ed.) (1994). *Identity Politics and Women Cultural Reassertion and Feminisms in International Perspectives*. San Francisco: Westview Press.

Mukherjee, Bharati (1994). *The Holder of the World.* London: Virago.

Mukherjee, Tutun (Ed.) (2006). *Staging Resistance: Play by Women in Translation.* New Delhi: Oxford University Press.

Nagarwala, Arati (1996). *The Bait.* Calcutta: Writers Workshop.

Nahal, Chaman (1995). *The New Literatures in English*. New Delhi: Allied Publishers.

Naik, M.K. and Narayan, S.A. (2001). *Indian English Literature 1980-2000: A Critical Survey*. New Delhi: Pencraft International.

Naik, M.K. and Mokashi-Punekar, S. (Eds.) (1977). *Perspectives on Indian Drama in English*. Madras: Oxford University Press.

Nanda, B.R. (1976). *Indian Women: From Purdah to Modernity*. Delhi: Vikas Books.

Narayan, U. (1997). *Dislocating Cultures: Indentities Traditions and Third World Feminism.* New York: Routledge.

Narasimahajah, C.D. and Srinath, C.N. (Eds.) (1999). *Drama as a Form of Art and Theatre*. Mysore: Dhvanyaloka.

Natalle, Elizabeth J. (1985). *Feminist Theatre: A Study in Persuasion*. Metuchen: Scare Crow Press.

Nayak, N. (1998). *The Struggle Within the Struggle*. Trivandrum: Programme for Community Organization Centre.

Nehru, Rameshwari (1950). *Gandhi is My Star*. Patna: Pustak Bhandar.

Neuman, Erich (1955). *The Great Mother: An Analysis of the Archetype*. Trans. Ralph Manheim. Princeton: Princeton University Press.

Omvedt, Gail (1990). *Viloence Against Women: New Movements and New Theories in India*. New Delhi: Kali for Women.

____ (1993). *Reinventing Revolution: New Social Movements and the Socialist Tradition in India*. NewYork and London: M.E. Sharpe.

Padmanabhan, Manjula. (1997). *Lights Out*. Included in *City Plays*. New Delhi: Seagull Books, 135-90.

____ (2001). *Harvest* in *Postcolonial Plays: An Anthology*. (Ed.) Helen Gilbert. New York: Routledge, 217-49.

Pillai, G. Sanskara (Ed.) (1986). *The Theatre of the Earth is Never Dead*. Trichur: University of Calicut.

Porter, E. (1991). *Women and Moral Identity*. Sydney: Allen & Unwin.

Prasad, B. (2009). *A Background to the Study of English Literature*. Madras: Macmillan.

Probyn, Elspeth (1993). *Sexing the Self: Gendered Positions in Cultural Studies*. London & New York: Routledge.

Rabate, Jean-Michel (Ed.) (2003). *The Cambridge Companion to Lacan*. Cambridge: Cambridge University Press.

Ramanujam, Renga P. (1996). *Marxism, Ideology and Literary Criticism*. New Delhi: Manak Publications.

Randive, V. (1987). *Feminists and the Women's Movement*. New Delhi: All India Democratic Women's Association.

Rehana, S. (1998). *Women in Indian Society*. New Delhi: Sage Publications.

Rice, Philip and Waugh, Patrica (Eds.) (2001). *Modern Literary Theory:* New York: Oxford University Press.

Rich, Adrienne (1979). *On Lies, Secrets, and Silence: Selected Prose, 1966-1978*. New York: Norton.

____ (1995). *Of Woman Born: Motherhood as Experience and Institution*. New York: Norton.

Richman, F.P., Swann, D.L. and Zarilli, P.B. (Eds.) (1995). *Indian Theatre: Tradition and Performance*. New Delhi: Motilal Banarasidas Pub. Ltd.

Richards, J. (1982). *The Skeptical Feminist: A Philosophical Enquiry*. Harmondsworth: Penguin.

Robertson, Roland (1995). *Globalisation: Social Theory and Global Culture*. London: Sage.

Roose-Evans, James (1989). *Experimental Theatre*. London: Routledge.

Russ, Joanna (1984). *How to Suppress Women's Writing*. London: Women's Press.

Ruthven, K.K. (1984). *Feminist Literary Studies: An Introduction*. Cambridge: Cambridge University Press.

Sangari, Kumkum and Sudesh Vaid (Eds.) (1990). *Recasting Women: Essays in Indian Colonial History*. New Brunswick: Rutgers University Press.

Sarabhai, Bharati (1943). *The Well of the People*. Calcutta: Vishva-Bharati.

____ (1952). *Two Women*. Mumbai: Hind Kitabs Ltd.

Sargent, Lynda (Ed.) (1981). *Women and Revolution: A Discussion of the Unhappy Marriage of Marxism and Feminism*. Cambridge: South End Press.

Sarkar, S. (1997). *Writing Social History*. New Delhi: Oxford University Press.

Schechner, Richard (2003). *Performance Theory*. London: Routledge.

Schreiner, Olive (1911). *Women and Labour*. London: Unwin.

Scott, Martin B. and Lymn, Stanford M. (1975). *The Drama of Social Reality*. New York: Oxford University Press.

Segal, L. (1988). *Is this Future? Female Troubled Thoughts on Contemporary Feminism*. London: Virago.

Sengupta, Poile (2010). *Women Center Stage: The Dramatist and the Play*. New Delhi: Routledge.

Sharma, K.K. (1977). *Indo-English Literature*. Ghaziabad: Vimal Prakashan.

Shepherdson, Charles (2000). *Vital Signs: Nature, Culture, and Psychoanalysis*. New York and London: Routledge.

Showalter, Elaine (1989). *Sister's Choice: Tradition and Change in American Women's Writing*. London: Oxford University Press.

Shiva, Vandana (1989). *Staying Alive: Women, Ecology and Development*. New Delhi: Kali for Women.

Shulamith, Firestone (1970). *The Dialectic of Sex: The Case for Feminist Revolution*. New York.

Skura, Meredith Anne (1981). *The Literary Use of Psychoanalytic Process*. Haven: Yale University Press.

Spelman, E. (1982). *Inessential Woman: Problems of Exclusion in Feminist Thought*. Boston: Beacon Press.

Spivak, Gayatri, C. (2006). *In Other Worlds: Essays in Cultural Politics*. New York: Routledge.

____ (1982). Foreword. *Writing and Sexual Difference*. Ed. Elizabeth Alge. Great Britain: Harvest Press.

____ (1990). *The Post-Colonial Critic: Interviews, Strategies, Dialogues*. Ed. Sarah Harasym. New York: Routledge.

Spacks, Patrice Meyer (1975). *The Female Imagination*. New York: Knopf.

Steedman, Carolyn (1986). *Landscape for a Good Woman*. London: Virago.

Styan, J.L. (1981). *Modern Drama in Theory and Practice*. Vols. 1 to 3. Cambridge: Cambridge University Press.

____ (1993). *The Elements of Drama*. New York: Press Syndicate.

Subramanyam, Laksmi (Ed.) (2002). *Muffled Voices: Women in Modern Indian Theatre*. New Delhi: Shakti Books.

Sunder Rajan, Rajeshwari (1993). *Real and Imagined Women: Gender, Culture, and Postcolonialism*. London and New York: Routledge.

Tendulkar, Vijay (1992). *Five Plays*. New Delhi: Oxford University Press.

Tharu Susie and Lalitha, K. (1993). *Women Writing in India*. Vol. II. New York: Feminist Press.

Thorne, Barrie and Henley, Nancy (1975). *Language and Sex: Difference and Dominance*. Rowdley Mass: New Bury House.

Thorne, B.C. Karamare and N. Hehley (Eds.) (1983). *Language, Gender and Society*. Cambridge: Newbury House Publishers.

Todd, Susan (Ed.) (1984). *Women and Theatre: Calling the Shots*. London: Faber and Faber.

Tompkins, Jane (1992). *West of Everything: The Inner Life of Westerns*. New York: Oxford University Press.

Tong, R. (1989). *Feminist Thought: A Comprehensive Introduction,* Ist Edition, London: Unwin Hyman.

____ (1993). (Ed.) *Feminist Thought: A More Comprehensive Introduction*. Sydney: Allen & Unwin.

Tuana, Nancy *et al.* (Ed.) (2002). *Revealing Male Bodies*. Bloomington: Indiana University Press.

Uberfeld, Anne (1999). *Reading Theatre*. Canada: University of Toronto.

Varadpande, M.L. (1992). *History of Indian Theatre. Lok Ranga. Panorama of Indian Folk Theatre*. New Delhi: Abhinav Publications.

Vatsyana, Kapila (1980). *Traditional Indian Theatre: Multiple Streams*. New Delhi: National Book Trust.

Verghese, Paul (1971). *Problems of the Indian Creative Writer in English*. Bombay: Somaiya.

Verschueren, Jef (1999). *Understanding Pragmatics*. London: Arnold.

Vogal, Lise (1984). *Marxism and the Oppression of Women: Toward a Unitary Theory*. New Brunswick, NJ.: Rutgers University Press.

Walby, Sylvia (1997). *Gender Transformation*. London: Routledge.

Wandor, Machelene (1981). *Understudies*. London: Routledge.

____ (1987). *Look Back in Gender: Sexuality and the Family in Post-War British Drama*. London: Methuen.

____ (1993). *Drama Today: A Critical Guide to British Drama 1970-1990*. London and New York: Longman.

Watson, G.J. (1983). *Drama: An Introduction*. London: Macmillan Education.

Weedon, Chris (1985). *Feminist Practice and Poststructuralist Theory*. Cambridge: Blackwell.

Weeks, Kathi (1998). *Constituting Feminist Subjects*. Ithaca New York: Cornell University Press.

Whelehan, I. (1995). *Modern Feminist Thought*. Edinburgh: Edinburgh University Press.

William, Raymond (1975). *Drama in Dramatized Society* (an inaugural lecture). Cambridge: Cambridge University Press.

Williams, Raymond (2006). *Drama in Performance*. New York: Basic Books.

Young, Kite (1993). *Planning Development with Women: Making a World of Difference*. London: Macmillan.

Zarilli, Philip (1984). *The Kathekalli Complex: Actor, Performance, Structure*. New Delhi: Abhinava Publications.

Journals and Periodicals

Agarwal, Bina (1994). "Positioning the Western Feminist Agenda: A Comment." *Indian Journal of Gender Studies*. 1(2): 249-56.

Akerkar, S. (1995). "Theory and Pracitce of Women's Movement in India." *Economic and Political Weekly*. 30(17): 2-24.

Banerjee, Sumantha (1983). "String of Betrayal". *Economic and Political Weekly*. 5 (Feb.): 175-77.

Bhatta, S.K. (1980). "Indo-English Women Playwrights". *Triveni,* 49.1 (April-June): 39-45.

Blake, Harry, Jardine, Alice and Kristeva, Julia (1981). "Women's Time." *Signs* 7(1) (Autumn): 13-35.

Burns, Pablo and San, Mae Lucy (2005). Women and the Changing World on Alternative Global Stage: Sixth Women Playwrights International Conference." *Asian Theatre Journal.* 22(2) (Autumn): 324-33.

Chandan, Mini (1999). "The Panotic Living Room in Manjula Padmanabhan's *Harvest*". *Journal of Literature and Aesthetics.* 7(1) (Jan.-June): 86-89.

Chandrashekhar, K. (1998). "All That is Gold does not Glitter." Rev. of *Harvest. Indian Review of Books.* 7(6) (March-April): 4-5.

Delphy, Christine and Danie'le L'eger (1980). "Debate on Capitalism, Patriarchy, and the Women's Struggle." (Summer) *Feminist Issues.* 1(1): 41-50.

Desai, Neera (1995). "The Making of a Feminist". *Indian Journal of Gender Studies.* 2(2) (September): 243-53.

Deshpande, G.P. (2002). "Theatre of Modernity. A Celebration of Modernity." *Theatre India.* 5(2) (May): 8-14.

Dharwadkar, Aparna (2006). "Review." *Feminist Review.* 84: 155-57.

Donovan, Josephine (1984). "Toward a Women's Poetics." *Feminist Issues in Literary Scholarship.* 3(1/2) (Spring-Autumn): 98-110.

Felman, Shoshana (1975). "Women and Madness: The Critical Phallacy". *Diacritics.* 5:4 (Winter): 2-10.

Garg, Mridula (1991). "Metaphors of Womanhood in Indian Literature." *Alternatives.* 16:4. (Fall): 407-24.

Gilbert, Sandra and Gubar, Susan (1980). "The Madwoman in the Attic: The Woman Writer and the Nineteenth Century Literary Imagination." *Nineteenth Century Fiction.* 35(2) (September): 225-29.

Gillepie, Pattie (1978). "Feminist Theatre: A Rhetorical Phenomenon". *Quarterly Journal of Speech*. 64(3): 284-94.

Hanrahan, Mair'ead (2004). "The Place of the Mother: Helen Cixous." *Paragraph*. 27(1) (March): 1-6.

Hasan, Anjum (1999). "Boay Blows: Women Violence and Survival: A Review." *Seasull Theatre Quarterly*. 2(24) (December): 85-87.

H.H. Annaiah, Gowda (1973). "Nissim Ezekiel's Plays." *The Literary Half-Yearly*. 14(1) (January): 11-16.

John, Mary (1996). "Gender and Development in India, 1970s-1990s." *Economic and Political Weekly*. 31(47) (Nov.): 3071-77.

Kaplan, Cora (1989). "Sea Changes: Essays on Culture and Feminism." *History Workshop Journal*. 27 (Spring): 200-06.

Kannabiran, K. and Kannabiran, V. (1991). "Caste and Gender: Understanding Dynamics of Power and Violence." *Economic and Political Weekly*, 26(37) (September): 2130-33.

Kazenstein, Mary Fainsod (1989). "Organizing Against Violence: Strategies of the Indian Women's Movement." *Pacific Affairs*. 62(1) (Spring): 53-71.

Krishnaji, N. (1980). "Lessons of Naxabari." *Economic and Political Weekly*. 15(36) (September): 1513-16.

Kristeva, Julia (2004). "Female Genius, Freedom and Culture." *The Earth Issue*. 2(2) (Autumn/Winter): 214-28.

Mackinnon, C. (1994). "Feminism, Marxism, Method and the State: An Agenda for Theory." *Signs*. 7(3) (Spring): 530-45.

Mitchell, Tony (1990). "Scritture Feminine: Writing the Female in the Plays of Dacia Maranini." *Theatre Journal*. 42(2) (May): 332-49.

Mukherji, Sumitra (1994). "Encounters with Cultures: Contemporary Indian Theatre and Interculturalism." *Seagull Theatre Quarterly*. 4: 3-12.

Mukherjee, Meenakshi (1995). "Literary History and the Politics of Gender." Review Article. *Indian & Journal of Gender Studies*. 2(1): 121-31.

Mykyta, Larysa (1983). "Lacan, Literature and the Look Woman in the Eye of Psychoanalysis." *Substance*. 12(2): 49-57.

Naik, M.K. (2001). "Cindrella Still: Recent Indian English Drama" *Littcrict*. 27(1:2) (June-Dec.): 34-42.

Padmanabhan, Manjula (1998). "A Nightmare Interview." *Indian Review of Books*. 7(6) (March-April): 5-6.

____ (1992). "A Government of India Undertaking." *In Other Words: New Writing by Women*. New Delhi: Kali for Women: 1-24.

Pravinchandra Shital (2007). "The Third-World Body Commodified": Manjula Padmanabhan's *Harvest*. *e-sharp*. Issue 8: 1-17.

Rabine, Leslie W. (1977). "Julia Kristeva: Semiotics and Women." *Pacific Coast Philosophy*. 12 (October): 41-49.

Raman, Vasanthi (2001). "The Women's Question in Contemporary Indian Politics." *Asian Journal of Women Studies*. 7(2): 39-71.

Scheper, Hughes, N. (2004). "The New Cannibalism: A Report on the International Traffic in Human Organs." *New Internationalist*. 300: 14-17.

Showalter, Elaine (1993). "American Gynocriticism." *Oxford Journals*. 5(1) (Spring): 111-28.

Tharu, S. and T. Niranjana (1994). "Problems for a Contemporary Theory of Gender in India." *Social Scientist*, 22 (March-April): 232-60.

Wilson, Edwin. (1987). "Separate and Subversive." *Wall Street Journal*. 23 (Sept): 32.

Yarbro-Bejarano, Yvone (1986). "The Female Subject in Chicano Theatre: Sexuality, Race and Class." *Theatre Journal*. 38(4) (December): 389-407.

Webliography

http://www.awtheatre.org

http:// www.centraltheatreartsacademy.org

http://diamondheadtheatre.com

http://erupkatha.com

http://www.googlebooks.com

http://www.hawaiishakes.org

http://www.ohilia.org

http://www.jstor.org

http://www.wju.edu.in

Index